D1380583

Christian Experience

Christian Experience

A selection of sermons of
Donald MacDonald
(Free Greyfriars, Inverness)

The Banner of Truth Trust

THE BANNER OF TRUTH TRUST
3 Murrayfield Road, Edinburgh EH 12 6EL
PO Box 621, Carlisle, Pennsylvania 17013, USA

★

© Mrs Margaret MacDonald 1988
First published 1988
ISBN 0 85151 527 4

★

Typeset in Plantin 10½/ 12 pt at
The Spartan Press Limited, Hants
and printed and bound in Great Britain
at the University Printing House, Oxford

CONTENTS

BIOGRAPHICAL INTRODUCTION

Donald MacDonald was born in the village of Cross in Ness on July 25, 1910. Ness is one of the more populous of the many country districts of the Island of Lewis, a spiritually-favoured island in the Outer Hebrides, off North-West Scotland. He was the child of a Christian home at a time when the general spiritual climate was one of apathy, if not ungodliness, despite the fact that church-going was near universal among adults. Though there were many fine Christians in the congregations of the Island, a spiritual malaise hung over that area of Lewis. Few young people went to church, in part because the prevailing poverty denied the children the clothes in which they could attend church services without embarrassment. When a revival broke out in the South Lochs area of Lewis in the early 1930s some of the young converts had never been to church before.

Much of this spiritual torpor had prevailed in Donald MacDonald's home congregation of Ness. Then in 1921, eleven years after his birth, a young minister was ordained and inducted to the pastoral charge of that huge congregation belonging to the Free Church of Scotland. Under the ministry of the Rev. Roderick John MacLeod a great spiritual movement ensued so that by 1924 the whole area was 'caught up' in revival. It was at this time that the special evangelistic services which are still held in the winter months and known locally as *orduighean beaga* were initiated in the congregation.

One of the many converts in Ness was Donald MacDonald, then in his very early teens. At the age of 14 years and 9 months he sought admission to the Lord's Table on the basis of his profession of faith in Christ as Saviour. When he appeared before the Kirk Session there was considerable reluctance on their part to grant him the privilege he sought. This may come as something of a surprise for us today who have become so accustomed to seeing many young converts professing their faith in Christ. But in the early 1920s converts of Donald's age were few and far between, and the older generation of Christians received with no little scepticism claims of conversion from one so young. This suspicion came to light at the meeting of the Kirk Session and it was only the intervention of one of the senior elders, Donald Murray, that moved the Session to grant the request.

Perhaps the treatment meted out to such a young convert contributed to the sensitivity of spirit that was such a characteristic of Donald MacDonald. He never quite overcame the hurt he endured at that early stage of his Christian life. Many years afterwards he was to make, in an unpublished sermon, this revealing autobiographical reference:

Many people think that to doubt is an evidence of grace. God's Word assures us that it is not an evidence of grace and it should never be taken as such. Now this is particularly true of West Coast people. I know this to my cost. When I was a young Christian – it was during a time of revival under the ministry of the late Rev. Roderick John MacLeod – there were lots of young people converted in that revival, and we were as happy as the days were long. The sun of God's favour was shining on our tabernacle and we were full of the joy of the Lord. But there were the older people, and many of them would say to us, 'Ah, but you wait'. When they spoke to us, you would never get them to say that they were sure of their salvation. They would say, 'We'll never be sure until we reach the other side, until we're taken into heaven'. And to my shame, I confess that they bent us to their own way of thinking – and to this day, on many occasions, I can hardly shake myself out of it. That kind of thinking has followed me, like a shadow, all my life. I owe to these dear old people, who have long since gone to glory, a debt that I can never tell, but I maintain, that in that particular aspect they were wrong. They maintained that if you were sure of your interest in Christ, there was something wrong with you, and that if you doubted your interest in Christ then that was an evidence of grace. I am sure that they were absolutely mistaken, but that attitude is characteristic of the Highland way of Christian living, and particularly of the West Coast.

Now that is a most interesting statement and it highlights two things. First, it seems to indicate that even as a young Christian Donald was confident in his own convictions. His opinions never rested upon the views of a majority, a fact which in later years sometimes gave him a reputation for being autocratic. But, secondly, it also tells us that *some* of the older generation did not take kindly to any expression of the assurance of salvation from

[viii]

one so young in the faith. During the course of his own preaching ministry Donald MacDonald could be devastatingly critical of any attempt to equate doubting of our salvation with spiritual depth of thought or development. That criticism was obviously rooted in the experiences he himself refers to in that quoted extract.

The young convert of the Rev. 'Roddy' John MacLeod feasted under the deeply-spiritual ministry of that greatly-used servant of God. It was, therefore, a source of profound sorrow for both young and old in Ness when their gifted minister left for another charge in 1927. Donald was then seventeen, having become a communicant member of the congregation in March 1925.

Donald MacDonald left Lionel Junior Secondary School in 1926. For four years he suffered the indignity of unemployment, ultimately securing work in the slate quarries at Ballachulish in Argyll. Accommodation for the workers was provided in communal huts. He was the youngest member of his particular hut and the only Christian. By God's grace he was able to witness to his fellow workers. He conducted worship each evening before retiring, although, inevitably, many sneered. Others, however, listened as God's Word was read and His name invoked, and they came to respect the young man who was not afraid to own his Lord. That disposition of 'fearing the face of no man . . .' continued with him and was probably forged in the difficult circumstances of that communal existence. When he became a minister, though he faced congregations fearlessly, he was no stranger to the 'butterflies' which often left him being physically sick before he entered the pulpit. How daunting is the most glorious of all vocations!

At about the age of twenty-three Donald MacDonald responded to the Lord's call to the ministry. His studies at University were followed by the usual three-year theological course in the Free Church College in Edinburgh. These studies were interrupted when, during a period of service for the Church in Prince Edward Island, the outbreak of the Second World War meant that he could not get back to begin his second year in College. On the advice of the Training of the Ministry Committee, he studied for one year in Knox Theological College, Toronto, at the same time conducting services in the Free Church congregation in that city. While there news reached him of his father's death in Lewis; the grief which this caused him was compounded by his inability to be at home to comfort his sorrowing mother and sister. Late in 1940 he was able to resume his studies in Edinburgh. The following year he was licensed to preach the Gospel, and thereafter ordained to the ministry and inducted to the pastoral charge of Urray in Easter Ross, in succession to R. A. Finlayson who was ultimately to become Professor of Systematic Theology in the Free Church College.

In January, 1942, he married Margaret Campbell who hailed from his native parish of Ness. Two sons, Murdo in 1943 and Roddy in 1946, were born to them in Urray.

In 1958, Mr. MacDonald was called by the congregation of Greyfriars, in Inverness, the capital of the Scottish Highlands. This charge had stemmed from a Free Presbyterian background and had been granted admission into the Free Church in 1957.

The decision to accept this call was not an easy one for him and with respect to that period in their lives his wife has written:

I remember most vividly the day he received the call to Greyfriars and how for weeks he agonised in prayer to God to reveal to him what he should do. On a Monday morning, the day before the Presbytery was due to meet to dispose of the call, he said to me after the boys left for school: 'I must decide today what to do about this call. I am going to the study to bring this matter to God in prayer and you do your duty here in the kitchen'. I tried to pray as earnestly as I could. In about a quarter of an hour I heard his footsteps coming from the study to the kitchen where he told me he was going to accept the call. I asked him how he came to that conclusion. He replied, 'I know my Bible quite well and I was never in the habit of opening it at random but this morning when I went into the study that is what I did, and the portion of Scripture that caught my eye was Acts chapter 10, verses 19–20: "Behold three men seek thee. Arise therefore and get thee down and go with them doubting nothing".'

There were just a handful of people attending Greyfriars, not more than 60, and the congregation was £7000 in debt. An appeal was made in *The Monthly Record*. In two years the money was paid. He felt so grateful to the Lord that he wanted to do something as a thank offering to Him. He said to me one evening while we were sitting together, 'What about getting a few thousand tracts and giving one to every house in the town?'. He there and then got up and and wrote a letter to the Christian Bookshop in Kilmarnock for samples. He said to me, 'This is going to cost us money and the congregation can ill afford it'. So the letter was put on the mantelpiece to be posted in the morning. That same evening a lady belonging to the congregation came to visit us. Before she left she handed Donald an envelope saying, 'I had a property in Glasgow that I sold recently so I decided to give some of the proceeds to the congregation'. The envelope contained £100, more than enough to pay for the tracts. 'Before they call, I will answer'. To this day some of the young folk in the congregation distribute tracts around the town.

Without question, Mr. MacDonald's new situation was a great challenge. While he took such practical steps as organizing tract distribution to reach outsiders (which went on week by week), and was himself a constant visitor to many homes, his main priority was the preaching of the Word, supported by earnest prayer. Under his care, the congregation developed into one of the largest on the mainland, its spiritual vitality being a testimony to an evangelical ministry which was in great demand throughout the Free Church. The nineteen-year ministry which he exercised in Inverness was without doubt the most fruitful of his life. Aware of the many difficulties which the newly-emerging congregation faced, he threw himself into the work with total commitment and his dedication bore fruit. The congregation began to flourish and his powerful preaching drew many hearers.

In 1972 Mr. MacDonald was unanimously nominated to the Moderatorship of the General Assembly of the Free Church. In carrying out his Moderatorial duties he justified the confidence shown by the brethren in proposing him for the highest honour that it is the Church's power to bestow. When he suffered a heart attack at the end of 1972 there was very general concern and sorrow, both in Inverness and far beyond. A fragment of Mr. MacDonald's personal diary survives from the subsequent days which he spent in Raigmore Hospital, and it gives us a glimpse of his inner life:

Monday, January 1, 1973. In Raigmore Hospital. Feeling very peaceful and happy. Like righteous Job my soul is grieved at the filthy conversation of some of the patients. O their blindness which makes them do it!

Rev. John MacLennan took service at 11 a.m. Text, 'Ye have not passed this way heretofore'.

Tuesday, 2nd Jan. Slept well. Pain gone away from my chest. Had a visit from Dr. Black, the house doctor, which greatly encouraged me. Evidently damage by thrombosis not severe.

Margaret called in afternoon and in evening she and M. (K) called. God was with us I believe, for they are both true children of God. Others also from all over are remembering me in prayer.

Wed, 3rd. Slept very well. Have been having times of sweet communion with a Mr. Tom MacLeod, a Free Presbyterian from Gairloch. He is a truly gracious man and I am glad to have got to know him.

Mr. Angus MacLeod called in afternoon. God be thanked for the quality of my elders!

In evening Marg and K. called. It was pleasant and touching and I believe a holy moment.

After eleven days in hospital, Mr. MacDonald returned home with the assurance that if he was quiet and careful for three or four months he should be able to resume a normal life. The enforced inactivity was not something to which he was accustomed. He read more than usual at this time, including P. B. Power's *A Book of Comfort, For Those in Sickness*, which he advised the Banner of Truth Trust to republish,[1] and he also returned to a favourite Puritan, Stephen Charnock, of whom he said on one occasion, 'There is none of the Puritans that I find so good for heart and head as Charnock'.

He wrote to a friend on February 8, 1973:

I feel very well and am up and about every day now. I am allowed out for short walks on a warm, calm day. But I am not allowed to do anything, not even to go to church. Both my own doctor and the specialist physician are adamant on my avoiding anything that might cause the least excitement. They just ignore me when I say that going to church to listen will not excite me. So I am afraid that I shall be a virtual prisoner until about end of March.

However, God has given me grace to be patient. I can see the working of His all-wise mind and hand, and I have thanked Him with all the sincerity I am capable of for laying His hand on me when He did. He made His own Word wonderfully precious to me, so precious that when I was in hospital and since I came home there were many occasions when I esteemed His Word more than my necessary sleep.

Now that I am getting better I hope I shall not be ungrateful and forget Him who was so kind to me in every way.

[1]His advice was followed and the book reprinted in 1974. In its republishing work the Trust used several volumes from Mr. MacDonald's own library. These included W. G. T. Shedd's two volumes, *Sermons to the Natural Man* and *Sermons to the Spiritual Man*, Charles Hodge on *Corinthians* and a number of Spurgeon's *Metropolitan Tabernacle Pulpit*. The Trust often benefited from his help and advice.

Biographical Introduction

Three full years of further fruitfulness, in which he was as active as ever, followed this heart attack. A letter to his people, appended to the Annual Financial Statement for 1976, gives an indication of the evident enjoyment of spiritual things which was marked in the congregation:

It is not presumption on our part to infer from your liberality and regular attendance on the public means of grace that the Holy Spirit has not departed from us. It is a great joy to see that the solemn obligations laid upon us in regard to the house of God are not forgotten. It is the gathered company of earnest, prayerful souls that gives the place its character. As we meet from week to week, we are conscious of an atmosphere that is charged with blessing, and sometimes the hours we meet together seem weighted with a joy too precious for this earth. Let us continue in earnest prayer that 'holy oil' will be poured upon us and spread to every home and every soul belonging to us. We thank God for everyone brought to the feet of Jesus, and for the abundant provision He lays to our hand to feed His sheep and lambs.

As has long been the case in the Scottish Highlands, communion seasons (when services conducted by a visiting preacher continue over a long weekend) are times anticipated with special eagerness. This was markedly the case in March 1977 when five new members were added to the congregation. The visiting preacher (the Rev. Murdo Alex MacLeod of Dingwall), on account of a bereavement in his own congregation had to return home before the service on the Monday morning, so Mr. MacDonald himself unexpectedly took that service in what was to be his final communion. His text was Matthew 13:51: 'Jesus saith unto them, Have ye understood all these things? They say unto him, Yea, Lord'. On the following Thursday he preached as usual at the congregational prayer meeting, when he took the words of John 6:67–68: 'Then said Jesus unto the twelve, Will ye also go away? Then Simon Peter answered him, Lord to whom shall we go? thou hast the words of eternal life.'

After preaching as usual the next Sunday (the evening sermon being included in these pages) he took a second heart attack on the following Tuesday. Once more recovery was anticipated as things seemed to be progressing smoothly, but his wish that he should die in harness – for he did not want to retire – was about to be fulfilled. On the evening of April 14, as his wife was preparing to go to the congregational prayer meeting he suggested that she should stay at home with him as he had several matters he wanted to discuss with her. She duly complied and sitting by his bedside received detailed instructions concerning his funeral service. Not given to any eulogizing of the dead, he insisted that the service would be as simple as possible, with Scripture readings, praise and two prayers. As he gave Margaret these details, he seemed to be reasonably well and, though somewhat distressed herself, she was not too apprehensive as she recalled his having done this kind of thing once before. During the night, however, Donald passed peacefully into the presence of the Lord whose name he loved to extol and for whose glory he longed.

The funeral service was conducted in accordance with his wishes on Monday, April 18th, 1977, in the presence of as large a funeral gathering as Inverness had probably ever seen, and his remains were lovingly laid to rest in Tomnahurich Cemetery. The congregation of Greyfriars erected a beautiful stone over his grave and a plaque on the wall of the church inscribed

In memory of a faithful preacher and beloved pastor . . .

★   ★   ★

Mr. MacDonald was a preacher of oustanding ability whose name will always be associated with his presentation of the evangel. His ministry in Inverness, for sheer spiritual blessing and growth, was probably without parallel in the Free Church of Scotland this century. Of course, the printed page cannot reproduce the power and the unction with which the sermons were delivered. One felt compelled to listen to him as the truth was expounded lucidly, powerfully and directly. He preached showing neither fear nor favour to any and he did so with the greatest acceptance in English and Gaelic.

He was not, of course, without his faults. Sometimes he was too independent in his actions and judgments but, as one of his office-bearers said in his life time: 'Though he is autocratic, his preaching is of such a high standard I can forgive him his autocracy!'

It was the all-consuming passion of his life to preach Christ and Him crucified. And his labours in that field were not confined to the pulpit. He was a pastor in the true sense of the word. His pastoral duties did not assume the appearance of mere social calling. He was always an ambassador of Christ in the home. His heart and prayers embraced every aspect of his people's welfare. He had a special attachment to the young. During his ministry he took great delight in mixing with and speaking to his young people, and his words of counsel to them in his 'Moderatorial Message' were typical of the man: 'Fill your mind now with the knowledge of who Christ is and what He has done for you and you are on the road to building up a rich and a strong character'.

There lay the strength of his own character. He was ever a debtor to the God who led him in his boyhood days to the knowledge of the Saviour, whom he served faithfully, always abounding in the work of the Lord. Though his services were in constant demand, he refused to become an itinerant minister and he was careful to devote most of his time and energies to the pastoral care of the people over whom the Lord had made him overseer.

Donald MacDonald never *wrote* a full manuscript for the pulpit. The contents of this book are sermons recorded on tape by one of his hearers. Arrangements were made for the transcribing and typing of the sermons. Much of the credit for that work goes to the Kirk Session of the Greyfriars congregation and, in particular, to its Clerk, Mr. Angus Macleod, referred to in the extract from Mr. MacDonald's diary. Indeed the earlier preparatory work of typing and editing was financed by the Deacons' Court of the congregation. The final selecting and editing were undertaken by the editorial department of the Trust.

These sermons will be valued, we believe, not only by those who heard him but by many others. MacDonald's type of preaching, in its simplicity, scripturalness and warmth, belongs to the same order as that of C. H. Spurgeon. Like Spurgeon he hid the extent of his knowledge in his preaching but his personal, well-used library was one of the best manse libraries in Scotland. Fellow ministers who came to stay with him, including Dr. Martyn Lloyd-Jones from London, always had the generous use of his books.

Prayer for revival was a fundamental part of Donald MacDonald's life. He died ignorant of the time when God will be pleased to send a further awakening, but he well knew what kind of preaching God has blessed in such eras. This book will surely serve to keep alive that same knowledge as well as encouraging Christians to continue in prayer.

MURDO ALEX MACLEOD

Stornoway, 1987.

[xv]

∾ I ∾

The Call of God

By faith Abraham, when he was called to go out into a place which he should after receive for an inheritance, obeyed; and he went out, not knowing whither he went.

Hebrews 11:8

My subject on this occasion is effectual calling as seen in the life of Abraham,[1] and, in particular, as attention is called to that life by the writer of the Epistle to the Hebrews. The difference between the Christian and the non-Christian, even though under the sound of the gospel, lies primarily in this, that a Christian has been effectually called. I would remind you of the words of Christ, when He said, 'No man can come unto me'. He did not say, 'No man will come unto me,' but, 'No man *can* come.' He has not got the ability. He is unable to do it 'except the Father draw him' (*John 6:44*). That is effectual calling and unless we have experienced the drawing of the Father, we are not, and cannot be, real Christians.

Abraham was an idolater just like the other people with whom he lived. In the providence of God he seems to have been a prosperous man. Then God called him to leave his native land and to go to a place that He would show him. Abraham obeyed God. We shall not engage in profitless speculation and ask why Abraham received such a call whereas others did not, nor shall we conjecture how God called Abraham, whether audibly, or in a vision, or by a dream. The Bible does not speak of these matters. As we consider, then, the call which Abraham received, we shall notice:

---

[1]Mr. MacDonald dealt so fully with the first head that he did not have time for the second and third.

1. Abraham received a sovereign call

The call originated in the will of God. It could not begin in the will of Abraham. God did not give the call to Abraham because Abraham was better than others. The plain fact is that we do not know why He gave it to Abraham. The answer to that lies with God. We cannot give it. And the same holds true of the effectual calling of God in every case. We do not know why God effectually calls one and not another. God willed it to be so and He willed it to be so even under the ministry of His own Son when He was here preaching on earth. Christ went about doing good, performing miracles, and declaring the truth of God. Some believed in Him and many believed not, but why this happened it is not for us to say, or to attempt to give explanations of these things. We know that the cause lies in the sovereign will of God and we dare not dispute the wisdom of God and the holiness of His will.

But you may say: 'I cannot fathom this; I cannot see how it conforms to reason; I cannot see how what you say can be reconciled with the responsibility which I am told I have.' To this I reply that if you try to give an explanation of these things in the light of your reason, it shows that you think far more of your reason than of what the Word of God says. These matters are far beyond the power of human reason and I am persuaded that they are beyond angelic reason also. They belong to the divine mind, they belong to God. As for reconciling the effectual call with man's responsibility I shall not attempt to do it. I could not do it. But there are two things of which I am absolutely certain; they are both revealed in the Bible with all clarity. I cannot reconcile them, but I know they are reconcilable. One of them is the sovereignty of God's work in the human soul. Man has got nothing to do with his effectual calling. He is entirely passive in that respect. The other matter is the absolute responsibility of my soul to God. I am as responsible to God as if everything depended upon myself. But you say, 'This does not make sense.' I reply that it does make sense, because this is the way it is; this is the way God ordered it to be.

Consider also that when God effectually calls a soul, that soul is convicted of its own guiltiness in God's sight, and accepts its responsibility before God and does not dispute it. The soul that is effectually called is conscious of its own responsibility. It is

[2]

convinced that its destruction is the work of its own hands, just as men and women in the day of Judgment will never dispute the verdict of God that consigns them to hell because they are workers of iniquity. They will not dispute that verdict. They will know that it is just. And when, in effectual calling, we are convicted of our sin, we are as conscious of our responsibility as unsaved sinners will be in the last day.

2. The effectual call is a divine call

It was the beginning of the work of God in the heart of Abraham and that is what made it effectual. In modern days there are many reasons why people may want to become professing Christians. And if religion becomes popular (as it once was in our land), if – by being religious, by being 'Christian', by sitting at the Lord's Table, by attending services regularly, we are more liable to receive worldly promotion – then many will be 'Christians' who are not Christians. Somebody once told me that in certain situations it is hopeless to expect promotion unless one belongs to the Freemasons. The result is that people who seek promotion are liable to become Freemasons. Now the same thing may happen with regard to the Christian faith. If the Christian faith were a sort of Freemasonry, and a method of getting worldly promotion, many people would become 'Christians' for that reason.

But such things do not explain why Abraham became a believer in the true God. It was not because he was discontented where he lived. People sometimes become discontented with the world; it becomes empty for them. They seem to prosper for the first part of their life and then, suddenly things begin to go wrong. Their loved ones begin to die, they themselves get aches and pains, and the world, as it were, goes flat. They lose their enjoyment of the world. They become absolutely discontented and say, 'What is the use of it all?' Examples of this are plentiful. How often we hear well-to-do people, popular actors and actresses, who achieve worldly fame, glory in themselves and their successes, but suddenly the bottom drops out of their world, and their riches, their mansions, and their popularity cease to please. That which constituted their 'life' now means nothing to them. Nothing at all! 'Vanity of vanities; all is vanity'!

[3]

It was not for this reason that Abraham became a believer. Nor did he become a believer because somebody suggested it to him. A believer cannot make any other person a believer. He may talk to another about Christ, but he cannot give him the effectual call. I grant that we can make believers of a sort. If we are stronger minded than others, we may without much difficulty make psychological believers of them. There are those who can make a person believe what is not true if he has the inclination to do so. Clever speakers can bring their hearers under certain mental pressures; they may even 'brain-wash' them, as the saying goes, and finally make them think that they are true believers. People ignorant of the truth of God may readily be caused to believe error about themselves.

A matter that has caused worry to many pertains to people brought up in Christian homes, always made to attend church, brought up to the reading of the Bible and to worship, and influenced to keep to all ethical aspects of the Bible. Later in life they question whether they are truly converted. They ask whether their faith is really genuine or merely the logical consequence of the way in which they have been brought up. Are they the subjects of a saving change or are they just the logical outcome of a Christian upbringing? I cannot answer that question. We know that there are many people who live like Christians, and who think they are Christians, and yet are not true Christians. And in a sense this is brought about by the good teaching they received in childhood and youth.

I remember an old man in my native place and nobody doubted the genuineness of his religion, but he himself was living in daily fear that he had no real faith at all. He had been brought up in a marvellous way at home, and he feared that all the religion he had in later life was destitute of saving faith. We are certainly to beware of making anyone believe that he is a Christian if he is not a Christian. We should never press people towards this kind of faith. We should press them as God presses them. We should tell them to strive to enter in at the strait gate; we should tell them to work out their own salvation with fear and trembling. We should tell them all that, but we should always leave the outcome in the hand of Him to whom it belongs, that is, in the hand of God.

I have had young people come to the manse and they would tell me that they were being pressed by friends in the congregation to go to the Lord's Table. Some of them were quite distressed about this pressure. This is a great pity. The matter of becoming a Christian is one that is purely between God and the individual soul. I agree that human instrumentality may be involved. A person could become a Christian today through my preaching. Many people have become Christians, I believe, through my preaching, just as the same thing happens through the preaching of others, but when a person becomes a Christian it is essentially the work of God in the soul of that person and there is no third party in the matter at all.

3. God's effectual call is an authoritative call

How did Abraham know that it was God who called him? He knew by the impression the call made upon his mind. He knew that it was not the voice of man even though he had never heard God's voice before. Compare Abraham's case with that of Levi, the publican. Levi was sitting at a table receiving taxes levied by the Romans on the Jews. This was his job. As he was engaged in this unpopular work, a Man who was passing by looked at him and said, 'Come, leave it all and follow me,' and immediately he obeyed the call. Why did that happen? What did Levi feel that made him act in this way? Again, think of two contented fishermen, James and John, who were mending their nets in their boat. The same Man passed by, and he said to them what seemed so ridiculous: 'Leave everything; leave your livelihood, and come and follow me. I do not make any promises. I will not give you houses or riches; but come and follow me.' Immediately they left their father and their boats and followed Him. Why did they do that?

Let me give you another such case. A certain man had dedicated his life to one thing, namely, the extinction of Christianity. One day, as he was pursuing his object and journeying to Damascus, he heard a voice from the heavens speaking to him, and immediately he answered, 'Lord, what wilt thou have me to do? Lord, I will do anything you want. What is it?' The Lord told him. We all know the kind of life he led from that day forward. Why did he become obedient so suddenly? How was his mind changed all at once? How, in a moment of time, did he become the very opposite of what he was when his journey began? What caused him to say, 'Lord, what wilt thou have me to do?' What caused him to become as different as light is from darkness?

All these changes came about by the authoritative call of God. That call of God persuades the reason. It moves the will. It affects the heart. It renews the whole man. When a person is called in this fashion he does not begin to ask questions about things that he cannot understand – the doctrine of election, human responsibility, and other things in the Bible that are so dark to him. These questions are never asked, for the call of God deals with his mind. It is an illuminating call and although it does not resolve all questions, it is so authoritative that the soul is drawn out in love to God Himself. Questions are shelved, all that is wanted is to do business with God.

4. The effectual call is a personal call

It was as personal to Abraham as if there was no one else in the world at the time but Abraham himself, as personal as if there were no other sinner in Ur of the Chaldees but himself. There is an 'aloneness' with God in effectual calling. I mean that when God calls you effectually, at that moment you would never know that there was anybody in the church but yourself; the whole of the preaching would be as personal to you as if only God and yourself were present. It is as personal as that! You would have no thought of people round about you; you would have no other thoughts about anything else but the fact that God was calling you, and that you were determined to obey the call of God. This is what happened to Moses when God called him. It was a personal call, and this is what makes one willing to leave all things and to bear the reproach that comes upon the people of God!

5. Again, the effectual call is a separating call

It separated Abraham from his former way of living. He was an idolater, but he was not an idolater after God called him. He worshipped God. He was separated unto God. Now no man is brought to this against his will; that is absolutely impossible. The will has to be renewed before the man is won. The effectual call of God convinces and draws the whole will of man, and so the man willingly separates himself from everything that is contrary to God. And this is Christianity. Sometimes people who say they are Christians ask: What is wrong with the doing of this or that? I expect you have heard the story of a lady of the last century who wanted to employ a safe driver for her horse-drawn carriage. Applicants came to see her and one man told her that he could go within such and such a distance of the edge of the road and that he could steer the carriage and the horses so well that there would be no danger of disaster. Another applicant said much the same thing, though in even stronger terms. A third applicant said that he could go to within an inch of the very edge even of a precipice but that he was such a good driver that no accident would occur. Then came a fourth man and the lady asked him how near he could go to the edge of a road without the carriage tipping over. He said, 'I do not know, Madam, I never tried. I always keep as near to the middle of the road as I possibly can, so that nothing undesirable will happen.' She said to him, 'I will take you to be my driver.' And when people begin to ask, 'How near the edge can I go? How much can I conform to the world? How worldly can I be, and still be a Christian?' they have never felt the effectual call of God. The effectual call of God makes you bid farewell to all things that border on ungodliness. All you want to do is to give yourself to Him.

There are various reasons for such a desire, but one of them includes all the rest. When God calls you effectually by His grace He gives you by faith to see the Lamb of God crucified, bearing your woe and sorrow and curse, bleeding on the tree. Once you see that, a million worlds would be to you as dung and trash, in comparison with His glory and mercy and grace. This is what makes a person who receives the effectual call fall in with that call. He does not raise questions. He is not like Lot's wife looking back to see the Sodom that had been left. In contrast, he looks unto Jesus, the author and finisher of his faith; Jesus who died for him on Calvary; Jesus who shed His blood; Jesus who gave Himself, and all that He was in God-hood and manhood, for his redemption. He now loves his Lord with all his heart and soul.

This does not mean that when a person becomes a Christian and separates himself from the world, that he takes up the attitude of 'Now I am far better than you are'. He does not look upon himself as being better than others, nor does it make him unfriendly towards people who are still unconverted. If he is working with them, he will be as friendly with them as ever he was; indeed, in one sense, more friendly. Nor does effectual calling make him a recluse. That sort of thing is hypocrisy. If people put on long faces once they become Christians and pretend that they are not interested in anything that pertains to their fellow men any more, and refuse to take any part, as they used to, in the ordinary talk and affairs of their fellow men, that is just simple hypocrisy. True Christianity does not have that sort of effect. It does not have any effect at all in respect of the desire to mix with people. Whoever mixed with people more than Jesus did? The Apostle Paul, speaking to the Corinthians, tells them to separate themselves from evil doers but he does not mean that they were to separate themselves from them in the literal sense. There are fornicators and idolaters in the world from whom you would want to separate yourselves, but not in the literal sense. To do that you must needs go out of the world. Paul says that he gave up all things for Christ, and counted them refuse in order that he might win Him, but in saying this, he is not talking about the dregs and the evil things of life, but about the good things of life. He is talking about things which were good in themselves, but if they kept him from Christ he separated himself from them.

The effectual call that came to Abraham made him poorer; it separated him from the world in that sense. Abraham never received one inch of the land that he was promised. Stephen tells us in the Acts of the Apostles that God 'gave him none inheritance in it, no, not so much as to set his foot on'. Not an inch did he get! And when his wife died Abraham had to buy a plot of ground in which to bury her. But God never gave him any of it. After taking him out of Ur of the Chaldees, and promising him, 'I will give thee this land and I will give it to thy seed after thee,' Abraham never owned one inch of it. And he became a poorer man than if he had stayed in Mesopotamia. But what of it? This is where the rich young ruler failed. Jesus said to him, 'Now you have your option; you have the option of following me and having your riches in heaven or staying with the riches that you have here in the world.' And the rich young man went away sorrowful, because he had many possessions.

But Abraham did not go away. And after all, what did he leave? What did he lose in comparison with what he gained? What did he gain obeying the voice of God? He gained the friendship of God, and that is of far more value than if he had owned the entire world. What will a man gain if he gets the whole world and loses his own soul? A man does not lose his soul when he gains the friendship of God. What did he gain here below? Did he not find the going difficult? God did not provide chariots for him. The road was long and testing, rough, difficult and dangerous – it was all that, and God did not put him in a chariot to take him to his destination. He had to make his own way under the guidance of God. What was it that kept him going? It was the same thing that keeps the Christian going through life – the call of God. Even if there were no other reward, the call of God, the drawing of God, the willingness of heart to follow God, and the joy of it all, more than compensates for anything lost in the process.

6. *The effectual call of God is an irresistible call*

Although that is so, if you want to do so, you can refuse the call of God upon your conscience and heart. Now does that make sense? How can a thing be resisted if it is irresistible? My meaning is this: that when God calls a person to salvation that person may at first try to resist.

Many persons have gone into the pub for the whole night long and drunk bottles of whisky in order to drown their sense of guilt, and to forget their conviction of sin. Some have gone to dances, and into all sorts of entertainment to enable them to get rid of the feeling they had that God was calling them. But they have failed, for God has winsomely and graciously persisted in drawing them to Himself. Their response to the call was not as speedy as in the cases of Levi, and James and John, yet it was the same winsomeness, the same effectiveness that accompanied the call in their case as in those of Christians mentioned in the New Testament. And so we learn the nature of God's call. It is an irresistible call even though it may for a time be resisted. Wherever God begins a good work, He carries it on, and He will never let you alone until at last you are brought to Himself.

But finally I would remind you of another sense in which some who hear God's call resist it. I mean this: that many people hear the call of God in their conscience and heart and they disbelieve it. Sometimes they are frightened by it; sometimes they seem to be attracted by it. But, in sum, they resist it. If they continue to resist, all it proves is that the call was not the effectual call. Had it been the effectual call they would have obeyed it. Here we come again to what I mentioned earlier – divine sovereignty and human responsibility. And I close with this word. If you are not called effectually, the responsibility is your own, not God's. Jesus said to the Jews, 'You will not come to me (you do not want to come to me) that you might have life.' In another place, this word 'come' closes the canon of the Scripture. 'The Spirit and the bride say, 'Come . . . And let him that is athirst come.' If we come, then we know that it is God who has called us to Himself for ever.

༄ 2 ༄

The Knowledge of God

For God, who commanded the light to shine out of darkness, hath shined in our hearts, to give the light of the knowledge of the glory of God in the face of Jesus Christ.

2 Corinthians 4:6[1]

The Second Letter to the Corinthians is one of the great expositions of the Apostle Paul, a letter that is full of marvellous teaching, and devotion to God. Christians can come to it over and over again and still find new things in it. And this is exactly what we are about to do today. Some of you may remember that I have preached on this particular text before, perhaps more than once. I remember that on one occasion my theme was on the action of God in giving light. God, who in the beginning commanded that light should shine out of darkness, is still doing the same thing, though in a different way in the hearts of people. I shall deal with this text today under a new aspect. That is why I make reference to the fact that I have preached on it before; for people may say, 'We heard him on that text before; why then should he preach from it again?' Why that assumption should prevail I cannot say, but I do know that some people think that a preacher should never preach more than once on the same text. If I were a really good preacher, if I lived near to God, and if I had a great mental ability like that of Baxter or Spurgeon, I could quite easily preach on one text all my life and bring new things out of it every time I did so. So rich is the Word of God! Those who talk in the way I have just mentioned merely betray their own ignorance of the richness of the Word of God. Some of us find that when we re-read familiar verses, or texts, they come to us with a new force and we see them in a new light.

[1]Preached on the morning of December 5, 1976.

And now, without any further introduction, let me mention three matters which I find in my text on which I would like to say a little to you today. Firstly, we read of the Source of Divine Light. Where does it come from? It comes from God. God has shined into our hearts. Secondly, What is the Matter of Divine Light? It is the glory of God and the knowledge of the glory of God. And thirdly, What is the Medium of Divine Light? It is the face of Jesus Christ. These are the three matters I shall try to open up.

I THE SOURCE OF DIVINE LIGHT

God has shined in our hearts. God is the source of divine light. No man can create even physical light except in the artificial way. People can light a candle; they can generate electricity; and these things are light, but they are not light in an ultimate sense and light in the ultimate sense is given only by God. It has been said that the most sublime sentence in the whole of the English language is to be found in the first chapter of Genesis: 'And God said, Let there be light': and there was light.' I once heard an English lecturer say that, of all the sentences in our language, nothing was more sublime than that third verse in the Book of Genesis. It is a marvellous statement: 'God said, Let there be light'. And what happened in the physical, natural creation happened in another way in the spiritual creation. We need light in the spiritual sense. The natural man is not only in darkness regarding the things of God, but he is in darkness himself. So terrible is our sin that we are in darkness. But we are not only *in* darkness. If a person is in darkness he can be taken out of it by somebody else, but if a person *himself* is darkness, what can be done? For example, if a person has no eyes, he is not only *in* darkness but he *is* darkness. And you and I cannot help him. If he were *in* darkness we could take him out of it but it is more than that. Man's sin is darkness itself. And in order to illumine man, God makes an external revelation of Himself, a revelation from the outside. He gives it in nature and He also gives it in the gospel.

This external revelation can be grasped by man's intellect; it can be grasped by human reason. A man can understand intellectually a tremendous amount regarding the gospel and the Christian religion. I suppose that is often true of those who are taught from week to week in the things of the gospel. Intellectually they can grasp much. On the other hand there are people who, for one reason or another – it may not be lack of intellect altogether – do not seem to grasp anything. Some people are in this plight for the simple reason that they are not interested. Some people, even in this congregation, do not know the ABC of the gospel of Jesus Christ. If you were to ask them the simplest question about the Bible, they just cannot answer. They may be far more intellectual than I am, but the point is, they are not as interested as I am. They do not listen, they do not study, they do not think. But if a person does think, and if a person is interested, then he can grasp much from the external revelation of God. The external revelation of God can change our minds to a tremendous degree. All morality comes from a belief in the external revelation of God.

But here in our text we read about the internal revelation of God. God shines in our hearts. What is meant here is a supernatural light, and that light no person can feel or can have unless it comes directly and specially from God. It does not matter how learned a person is, it does not matter how much he knows about classics or philosophy or English or any other subject under the sun, he is as blind and as ignorant regarding this internal light – the saving knowledge of God – as anybody else in the world. He is as blind as the very heathen, until supernatural knowledge comes to him from God. He cannot grasp the things of the Spirit of God. He can reason about them, he can argue about them, and very often these learned people do argue. There are things which they cannot reconcile, things which they cannot understand. But the point is, that no man or woman, boy or girl, can understand savingly and sanctifyingly the things of God until God intervenes and gives him or her light to do so. It is God and God alone who shines in our hearts, in a supernatural way with a supernatural light, to give us the light of the knowledge of the glory of God.

Now what is the main difference between the two conditions of the mind and heart? It is this. The external revelation of the gospel changes the outward life and may make people moral, but the internal revelation of the gospel changes people's hearts. There is a world of difference between a change of heart and a change of light. The two things are not synonymous. There can be a change of light without a change of heart. But there can be no change of heart without a change in the light. The supernatural light of God, and that alone, can change a heart, as in the case of Lydia whose heart the Lord opened, so that she was a different person for the rest of her life. The teaching of man, as I have said, is of no avail in this matter. I have often said to myself, and I suppose I am not alone in saying it, that I have wasted my years in my work among you when I see so little success. I often say, 'I wish I had gone away ten, twelve, fifteen years ago, so that somebody else could have come in who would have been more useful than I have been.' And I believe with all my heart that another person might have been much more useful. But then again, I tell myself that this is a very foolish thought. That another person might have been far more able, of that there is no doubt; but he could not have been more useful unless God made him so. Spiritual usefulness does not depend upon natural ability; it depends upon God and His application of the Word to people's hearts. The giving of light to hearers does not come from the man who preaches, but from God Himself.

Think of this, that even when God's Son, Jesus Christ, was in the world and taught His disciples, and, as man, explained the Scriptures to them, they did not understand. We have it crystal clear in the Bible, that although Christ, patiently, for three whole years taught His apostles, they did not understand many things that he taught them. Jesus says, 'Why do you not understand?' After the Lord's resurrection took place, the apostles at first did not understand and found it hard to believe that Jesus had risen from the dead. It was not that He had not told them plainly enough that he would rise again. The trouble was that they did not understand Him. And the reason for that was, that Christ as man taught them the Scriptures. He interpreted the Scriptures to them as man. Afterwards, however, He imprinted them on their hearts as God. Christ had a dual nature: as man He taught them the Scriptures and they did not understand them; later, as God, He imprinted them on their hearts and minds and *then* they understood them. That is the source of divine light. And let us, my friend, realize that no man – it does not matter who he is, it does not matter how intelligent he is, it does not matter how much he knows about other things – can know anything about the divine light until God shines into his heart. And no truth of itself can possibly make people understand until God imprints it on their minds.

[14]

The Knowledge of God

What is this? It is the glory of God, and the knowledge of the glory of God. Here we come to the brink of a vast ocean – the glory of God! One particular thing I want to say to you, at this point, and I say it to myself also. It is this. Try to pray for the help of God every day you live, so that everything in your life will become subservient to your knowledge of the glory of God. I do not say that you must acquire knowledge; teachers must teach themselves knowledge. Those in professions must bring and keep themselves up-to-date in their knowledge of modern medicine and modern science and such-like things. But let everything be subservient to this one pursuit; strive for the knowledge of the glory of God. Let that be your aim. Whatever else you know, get to know the glory of God. Other things can wait; you can afford to have less knowledge of earthly things, but not of Him.

What, then, is the glory of God? God has a glory, His essential glory, which He does not impart or reveal. But in our text we read of His revealed glory. He gives us the knowledge of that glory. Briefly, then, what is the glory of God of which we can have knowledge? It is astonishing, astounding, that we, miserable creatures, as we are, can *know* the glory of God, the eternal, Almighty God. We can know God, we can have knowledge of God, a supernatural knowledge of God, a knowledge of Him by the light He imparts and gives to our hearts. What is it, then?

It is the glory of His love. God is love, God loves sinners. You know that. But the question is: Do you know it intellectually, or do you know experimentally? Do you know it intellectually, as you know the sun is there, and when the sun is not shining? When it is shining you feel its warmth and you see its light, but when it is not shining you only know the fact of its existence, but you do not feel its warmth and light. Now then, do you know that God is love? Have you the knowledge of the glory of His love in your own heart, or have you merely got an intellectual apprehension of the matter? How do you answer my question? I cannot answer it for you. But all Christians have an experimental knowledge of the love of God. Oh yes, God loves us, we know He does, but it is not enough to know that intellectually. We must have the fulness of that knowledge in our hearts.

The glory of God is the mercy of God. Often you have heard me say that God can have mercy on the devil's companions, and that even if a person is, as it were, on the brink of hell, God can have mercy upon him. Many times you have heard me say that it does not matter how many sins a person has committed – as long as he has not committed the sin against the Holy Ghost – God can receive him into His bosom, as the father received the prodigal. That is the glory of His mercy! There is no limit to the mercy of God. I know that. I knew that from my early days, but do I know it in my own soul? Do I know the sweetness of it? Have I tasted the mercy of God in the forgiveness of my sins? Do I know that, great sinner though I am, the glory of the mercy of God will swallow up my sins and I shall be drowned, as it were for ever, in the glory of that divine mercy? Do I know this, do I have the knowledge of it for myself? In his Epistle, Paul is deeply concerned to impart to believers the knowledge of the glory of God.

Then again, there is the knowledge of the divine holiness. We are in no doubt that God is holy. God is holy, of purer eyes than to behold sin. But do I personally know that God is holy? Has he changed my heart and made me holy also? Do I behave in the light of the fact that God is a holy God? In my private life, my business transactions, my family life, in all aspects of my life, is it imprinted upon my soul that the Holy God is a consuming fire, and that His word runs, 'Be ye holy, for I am holy'. When I read a book, when I listen to a conversation, when I talk to other people, does this as it were imprint itself upon me, 'As He which hath called you is holy, so be ye holy in all manner of conversation'? Think of these things.

I must also make mention of the glory of God's government and of His power and of His wisdom, for these are included in what is meant by the light of the knowledge of the glory of God. And God brings these things into the hearts of believers, those who possess the knowledge of the glory of His love. People find fault with God because there is a hell, a place of punishment and torment for the lost. His Word speaks of the eternal flame where the worm dieth not, and the fire is not quenched. This I can say of the matter, that if I have the knowledge of the glory of God, I know this, that if God made a hell, God was right in doing so. And I know that if I am not saved, but sent to that hell for all eternity, God is right in sending me to that hell. God would be

[16]

just in doing so. This is the light of the knowledge and the justice of God. The glory of His judgment!

Oh, there is so much to say! Remember what Moses said to God when he came down from the mount. When he was on the mount he saw much of the glory of God; and he saw God face to face – whatever that means – but what did Moses say after it all? He said, 'Lord, show me thy glory'. After all that he had already experienced this is how he speaks! He knew that he could not of himself learn more of that glory unless God showed it to him, and that the more a man sees of the glory of the great Jehovah the more he wants to see. Think again of what Moses said, 'Lord, show me thy glory' – after seeing Him face to face! Remember, too, what John said quite early in his Gospel, when he was writing about the coming of the Lord Jesus into the world, 'We beheld his glory, the glory as of the only begotten of the Father, full of grace and truth.'

III THE MEDIUM OF DIVINE LIGHT

And now a word about the medium of the Divine Light, by which I mean that we see the glory of God in the face of Jesus Christ. But what does the face of Jesus Christ mean? It does not mean natural appearance. I have told you before that, for years, I believed and preached that because of His innocency and sinlessness, Jesus Christ was fairer in appearance than all other persons. But now I retract that thought. I honestly believe that it is not true. I believe that Christ's face was not any more beautiful than other faces. Think of the words of the prophet Isaiah, 'When we shall see him (the Messiah) there is no beauty that we should desire him.' Christ was made in all points like unto what we are, and I now hold that Christ's face had a quite ordinary appearance. There was nothing in it, any more than there was in Peter's face or John's face. What, then, does 'the face of Jesus Christ' mean? In a word, it is the gospel. If anybody asks you what is meant by the face of Jesus Christ, as we have it here in my text, and as we have it mentioned in other places in the Epistle, your correct answer will be: the gospel of Jesus Christ. We cannot have a more perfect account of God than we have in the gospel. As much is revealed of God in the gospel as the word can express. And in the gospel we see His glory.

[17]

We get the knowledge of His glory from the gospel, from the study of the gospel, and from the meditation of it. From our prayers regarding the gospel, we get the light of the knowledge of the glory of God. Here is the face of Jesus Christ.

As I close, there are certain things I want you specially to remember. First of all, do not go away with the idea in your mind: Oh, this knowledge is too strange for me, it is too high to understand. It is only for you, not for the likes of me. I say this to you, that whoever you may be, sitting in front of me here in your pew, this is within your range. You can reach it, you can get the light of the knowledge of God in the face of Jesus Christ. I want to tell you how this is possible. You can get it, first of all, by studying the Word of God. I was once listening to a man whom I did not know, and whom I had never seen before, and he gave an address, quite a long one, and it was a delight to listen to him. I made it my business after the meeting to find out where he got his knowledge. I said to him, 'Where were you trained?' and he replied: 'I was thirty-six years of age before I knew anything about God or about the Bible. It was a foreign book to me, but at the age of thirty-six I was converted and I spent three whole years in the study of the Bible. During these three years I did not know there was such a thing as a commentary on the Bible. I was apart for three whole years just studying the Bible. When I emerged and came out into the open, I discovered that what I had learned from the Bible was Reformed theology.' He had seen the glory of God in the face of Jesus Christ. And he had obtained the knowledge of the glory of God from the study of the Bible.

My friends, I shall not be with you for much longer. Death will overtake me, but will leave many of you after I am gone. I plead with you, study the Bible if you want to get the knowledge of the glory of God. Do not be content to come to church once or twice a Sabbath to hear the Bible read publicly. I plead with you, study the Bible, read it and study it for yourselves if you want to know Christ.

And the second thing is that I would persuade you to love God. His love generates love. When you get the knowledge of the glory of God, your heart will grow warm with love to God. You will adore God: you will not only admire the glory, you will adore Him. You will love Him with all your heart, He will win your heart. He will win your love.

And the third thing is: if you want the light of the knowledge of the glory of God, obey Christ, be obedient to Him. Say 'goodbye' to sin; bid it farewell for ever. And as for you, as you serve the Lord and are obedient to His Word, you will get fresh gleams of the glory of God instilled into your mind.

∾ 3 ∾

Trust in God

Behold, God is my salvation; I will trust, and not be afraid.

Isaiah 12:2[1]

This morning we meditated for a little time on what David said in Psalm 56:3: 'What time I am afraid, I will trust in thee'. In David's experience, as we saw, fear came first; fear filled his mind, but he knew what to do in that circumstance: he trusted in God. This evening I am taking the converse of David's statement as it is uttered by the prophet Isaiah who says, 'I will trust and not be afraid.' But I want to say at the very outset that the two statements are not contradictory. It does not mean that the prophet Isaiah was nearer to God than David was, or that he had more knowledge of Him. They are two different utterances, spoken no doubt under two different attitudes of mind. Being what we are, our minds change, and of course, when our minds are influenced by certain events and certain circumstances, we say what we think. That is what we find here.

David, at the time when he said, 'What time I am afraid, I will trust in thee' was really in a bad way. Everything was going against him. He seemed at last to be exposed to the fury of his enemies and he could see no way of escape. This, then, was his conclusion: There is nothing I can do.

> *No refuge, no safety in self do I see*
> *Jehovah Tsidkenu is all things to me.*

He trusted in God. Now, without going back to the things that I said this morning, I would remind you of the conclusion. I pleaded with the congregation to put their trust in God, whatever sense of sin they had. If you are afraid, if you are afraid of God Himself, if

[1]Sabbath evening, February 27, 1977.

[20]

you are afraid of Him as a righteous Judge, who will judge you at the
last day according to your works; if you are afraid of death and of
what will happen to you when you go into the next world; if you are
afraid of the resurrection or the Judgment, afraid of anything, trust
in God. That is it, friends; nothing else will give you peace. Try what
you like, nothing will give you peace, lasting peace, but trust in God.
Here in our text we have the prophet Isaiah saying, 'I will trust and
not be afraid'. This does not mean – cannot mean – that the prophet
was never afraid after he spoke these words. I do not want you to go
away with the impression that from the time he said these words the
prophet Isaiah went on his way without ever having any fear. I do
not think that is true in any Christian's experience, at least not from
what I infer from the Bible. I may be wrong, but this is my
interpretation of the Bible. I do not act upon anything I feel within
myself or even by anything anybody else has said to me. But I submit
to what the Bible tells me, and I think it is true to say that, generally
speaking, Christian people have their fears as they go through life.
And I do not think that Isaiah was any exception to this general rule.

Now the reason for which he said 'I will trust and not be afraid'
was the preceding clause: 'Behold, God is my salvation.' That was
the foundation stone that he laid, or rather, that was laid for him. If
a mason knows that he has laid a flawless foundation on a flawless
base he knows he can infer from that that the building he intends to
erect will be safe from collapse. Here then, is the foundation and
the foundation stone – 'God is my salvation'. No one else! *He* is my
salvation. If a person can speak in that way, why should he be
afraid? If God is his salvation he can trust his God – and he does. So
it is as easy as that, as clear as that – 'Behold, God is my salvation'.
Therefore the inference is: 'I intend to trust Him. I do trust Him
and I will not be afraid.' But you may ask, 'Did you not say that he
had his fears afterwards on occasions?' Yes, I suppose he had his
times of fear as do most other people, but at that particular time he
had none. Similarly there are times in Christian experience when a
person is not afraid because he can say without a shadow of a
doubt, 'Behold, God is my salvation'. Is that not what we read of
Paul in his Second Letter to Timothy – words written by a man on
the brink of the grave – 'the time of my departure is at hand . . .
Henceforth there is laid up for me a crown of righteousness which
the Lord, the righteous judge, shall give me at that day'? Paul had
already trusted God. God was his salvation and in consequence he

looked upon death with the greatest equanimity. He trusted in God and fear fled from him.

I WHAT IT IS TO TRUST

1. To trust is an attitude of mind

You trust consciously. You know what you are doing when you trust. To trust and to have faith – that is, to believe – are one and the same thing, at least more or less. It is difficult to explain. When John G. Paton went out as a missionary to the South Sea Islands, he spent most of his time in preaching and in translating the Bible into the native language. But he found that when he came to the word 'faith' he could not find a word in the native vocabulary to express it. Then one day, when he was in his room writing, one of his faithful servants and friends came in to him. He was sitting on a chair and had his legs up resting on something, and the man said to him, 'You are sitting with your legs up', and quick as lightning John G. Paton got the thought, 'I will take my legs down'. He did so, then leaned hard on the back of the chair and asked, 'What am I doing now?' The man said: 'You are leaning'. The word he used meant 'You are trusting yourself to the chair – to support you, to hold you up; the back of it keeps you from falling'. It was a most expressive word and Paton got up and shouted for joy that at last he had learned the word that was so essential to translate the Scriptures into the native language.

So this is the meaning of trusting: you lean exclusively without depending in the least upon any resources of your own. You have no other resources in any case. 'I will trust in God. I will trust without depending in the least upon anything else'. This morning I said to you, and I must say it again, that if ever I became conscious of real, absolute trust in God, without having trust in anything else, I feel I would be the happiest man on the face of God's earth. I hope it is true of me that I do so, and I hope it is true of you. But even when we come to trust in the blood of Jesus Christ we carry so much of our own false sufficiency with us. We carry so much of ourselves with us even in prayer, we mix so much of pride and self-sufficiency with our faith, that we are not really trusting as we ought. We are trusting, but not wholly, not as we ought to do, because we carry so much of this self-sufficiency with us.

[22]

Perhaps a perfect trust in God is quite impossible as long as we are in this life. Our imperfections apply to everything. If we were in charge of several hundred orphan children, and the house-keeper came and said to us at night, 'We haven't a crumb to give to the children in the morning', I wonder how many of us would trust in God so completely as to go to bed and have a good night's sleep, believing that, when the morning came, sufficient food would be in hand for several hundred children. That is what George Müller did more than once. He never lost his sleep over it at all, even when the cupboards were bare, and it was to him according to his faith. That is what I mean by trusting God entirely. But some people may say – 'Oh, well, Müller was a great man of God; he was a great man who spent a night in prayer, in agony; no wonder he got something in the morning.' George Müller did not do that. He did not trust in his own prayers. He did not stay up all night to pray that before the children rose in the morning somebody would come with sufficient breakfast for them. He trusted so exclusively and entirely in God that he put God before his own prayers. Yes, he was a great man, but what I mean to bring home to you is that he did not depend upon the time he spent in prayer; in a sense, he was always in prayer and he trusted God. He believed that God would keep His promises, and God did so, and George Müller lost no sleep over it. Well now, that is the attitude of mind that I am talking about.

The words 'I will trust, and not be afraid' indicate a holy determination. 'I *will* trust'. And why should you not trust? 'I will trust and not be afraid'. My friend, did God ever let you down? Did you ever trust and find Him untrue and unfaithful? No! Well then, if you trusted Him and found Him true, why will you not determine tonight by His grace to trust Him for ever? You may say, 'Things are against me; things are turning out quite contrary to my expectations.' But go on to say: 'I *will* trust and not be afraid; even if troubles come upon me, even if the waves threaten to swallow me up, I will trust and not be afraid. I know that all things work together for good to them who love God.'

Let us look again at the word 'trust'. To trust is the very first act of a new-born soul. 'I will trust.' Let me make the statement more personal. If you do not trust God for salvation, you are not a Christian. The first thing you do in becoming a Christian is to trust God absolutely for your salvation. You no longer trust in your own righteousness, in your own prayers, in your own good works. You trust God, you trust in the blood of Jesus who bore your punishment on the cross, and you believe that because Jesus bore the punishment you will not have to bear it. That is trusting God.

2. *The second thing I will mention about trust is that it is nothing but obedience to a command*

If anything is commanded frequently in the Bible it is to trust in God, and when you are doing it you are only doing your bounden duty. Trust in God. It is a command to the unbeliever and it is a command to the believer alike. It is God's command to us all.

3. *The third thing to observe is that trusting God is the chief way in which we can honour and praise Him in this world*

If we trust Him, then we praise Him and glorify Him and honour Him far more than we do with our works, although works are certainly important. But this is the chief way in which we can honour God – by trusting Him. Abraham trusted God when he went at God's command to offer up Isaac. He believed in God. He trusted God when He told him he would have a child in his old age. He trusted that what God said He would bring to pass, even against nature. So, my friend, if we trust God like that, if God says that the rivers will start running up the hills instead of running down, if God says that things will go against nature, that nature will act contrary to herself, if God says that the moon or the sun will stop in their course, if we truly believe God, then we shall not be confounded. God said some things to the men of strong faith which, humanly speaking, were absolutely incredible. Yet they believed, they trusted, and it was to them according to their faith.

4. *Take note that we trust when we have a sense of need*

A sense of our need in the sight of God should never leave us. I was greatly taken the other day in my Bible reading – I never noticed it before, I must confess – but I was greatly taken with the thought of a certain preacher that when Paul wrote the General Epistles – Romans, Corinthians, Ephesians and so on – to the churches, he always began by wishing them grace and peace. But when he wrote

[24]

the Pastoral Epistles – that is the Epistles to Timothy and Titus – he began by asking for them grace, *mercy*, and peace. And the preacher said, 'Why did the apostle ask that these men, who were great men in the church and pastors in the church, should receive mercy as well as grace and peace?' And being a preacher himself, his answer was that everybody needs mercy, but nobody needs it more than the preacher of the gospel. The higher your office, the greater your responsibility, the more are you dependent upon the mercy of God.

5. *Our trust in God is based on the promises of God*

But you say then: 'Where will I find and obtain the promises?' God does not speak to us as he spoke to Abraham.' We get the promises in the Bible. And the promises in the Bible are just as sure as if you heard God speaking them into your ears. Just as sure as that! They are just as sure as if God sent an angel from heaven with a message directly and specifically for yourself. If God says anything in His Word by way of promise, then it is sure. Now that is what you have to trust in. If God says that the blood of Christ cleanses you from all sin, then that is His promise and His promise is sure. So your trust is based upon the promises of God. And the promise of God is solemn and holy and it is even ratified by His oath. Oh, that is a marvellous thing that is said in the Epistle to the Hebrews (*chapter 6, verse 13*). Think of it, my friends! On one occasion God swore by Himself! When a person goes into a court and stands in the witness box he has to take the oath in the name of a greater than himself. He takes the oath on the Word of God. But God could not swear by anyone greater than Himself, so He swore by Himself, that the promise would remain for ever firm and sure.

What more do we want than that? Oh, it is a marvel! We must be strange creatures if we do not trust God. When you think that these words are words ratified by God's oath, taken upon Himself, how is it that some among us do not trust in God? God will not break His Word. He will not be unfaithful to His covenant. An English preacher, a remarkable man in his day, once said: 'I feel that I would not break a promise, not even if it were to the devil I made it. I feel that a promise is such a holy thing, it is such a wonderful thing, that it should stand in every circumstance. I would never break a promise, not even to the devil himself.' These are strong words, of course, but the man who uttered them was wanting to emphasize the faithfulness of God. He was saying that, if such were his own feelings about human promises, how much more firmly must God bind Himself to His promises!

What about the faithfulness of God regarding His own Word? If you are faithful, you would feel it a dishonour to go against your word given to a friend. How much more God! In other words, if we do not trust God it is the greatest dishonour we can put upon God. It is the greatest of sins. I am sure of this. If tonight you were to commit a theft, if you were to commit uncleanness, that would be bad enough, but it is not as evil in the sight of God as not believing Him. If a person came tonight to your house and broke in and stole things belonging to you, well, that also would be bad enough, but if a person said to you when you were telling the truth, the whole truth and nothing but the truth, 'I don't believe you' – that would be worse. The stealing of your goods did not discredit your character. It only deprived you of things belonging to you. But if a man says to you that he does not believe you, that casts dishonour on your character. He is discrediting your character. And when we do not trust God, when we do not act trust in Him, we are really disbelieving God, and saying, 'I do not believe you'. And so we go on in our own sinful way.

6. *Once again, to trust God means that we have every faith in His sufficiency*

We have every faith in His self-sufficiency, every faith that He will uphold us, every faith that He will provide for us, and every faith that He will comfort us. The Lord will provide, for His name is Jehovah-Jireh. Spurgeon tells in his own way of people who become anxious when they think that the Lord may not provide for them. He says that he once had a godly lady in his congregation and when he visited her she used to tell him of her constant fear that her needs would not be met as years passed by. There were no pensions in those days. She was living on whatever she had saved during her working life and, of course, it was getting less and less as the years moved on. And she said to Spurgeon one day: 'I am afraid that I will not have enough to bury me. You know, if I live till I am 80 I will have nothing.' 'But', says Spurgeon, 'she died when she was 70.' Her fears were groundless and so are ours in the times when we are tempted to believe that God will not provide, that we shall have needs that will be beyond the sufficiency of God to do anything about. All too often we measure God by our own poor resources, by our own inadequacy, and instead of going out of ourselves, and trusting Him entirely, we feel that God is somehow like ourselves. If we have not got this or that, He has not got it either. And yet He is Jehovah-Jireh. With heaven and earth at His command, He waits to answer prayer.

II TRUST AND FEAR

1. There are some who trust and are not afraid

'I will trust', said Isaiah, 'and not be afraid.' 'I will *not* be afraid.' At this point I want to go back to one or two things I said this morning. I said that frequently people are afraid, like David, of past sins. David had every reason to be afraid of past sins, for he committed sins and I am sure he did not forget them. Psalm 25 makes it very clear that he did not forget them. Man of God though he was, he committed sins, just like you and I do. Yet he said, 'I will trust and not be afraid.' He is sorry that he sinned but his trust in His merciful God casts out fear. He tells us to think of the matter in this way: if you have committed wrong and been fined or put into prison, once you have paid your fine or been released from prison, it is all over. The law is satisfied. Similarly, a truly Christian man laments his sins, his past sins, but he says: 'I will trust and not be afraid' because God's law has been satisfied. Christ has met all the demands of the law for my past sins and therefore I can say, 'I will trust and not be afraid.'

Let me quote Spurgeon to you once again. He says about himself that sometimes he felt his life to be 'as dark as hell's profoundest night'. Think of that! Such was the expression that he used and it is arresting enough for anybody to remember, but he goes on to say: 'I trust in my God and I know that His light will shine upon me, and I know that I shall never perish, nor will any man pluck me out of His hand.' Now, friend, tonight you may be bowed down, burdened because of your past sins. How are you going to get rid of that burden? There is only one way. Trust in the work of Jesus Christ! Believe that He died bearing the punishment of your sins; trust Him and then you will not need to be afraid. And you will not be afraid.

The truth is also the same regarding present things. Present things sometimes make us afraid. But still we have to trust God. And again I am not saying anything that is not true in Christian experience. It is of no use trying to think or to make out that we are different from other people. It is not so. We are more or less the same, whatever differences there are between us; in one sense we are all cast in the same mould. I remember hearing the late Professor John Murray saying on one occasion that sometimes certain thoughts came into his mind and that he thanked God that no one knew them nor would ever know them. I believe that Dr. Kennedy of Dingwall said something to the same effect. Well, friend, do not you say the same? You know the effect these thoughts have on you. You know how they cast you down with the gloom they bring into your soul, the blight that they cause. These things come in and they raise their own questions and cause you to say: 'Well, now, how can this be if I am right with God?' And the only answer is: 'I will trust Him, and not be afraid.'

I am not saying that you will get rid of all such thoughts. You will not get rid of them altogether, but you need not be afraid. Although these thoughts have come into your mind you need not be afraid of the Judgment. You are trusting God, and if you trust God you do not need to be afraid. It does not matter what is true of yourself; you trust what God is and what He said. 'I will not be afraid' – not in a carefree sort of way, but 'I will not be afraid', because I know that the element of faithfulness in the character of God will never be broken. Nobody can ever break in upon that, no circumstance can possibly alter it. It is not as if you have known God for twenty or thirty years during which He has never failed you, but that you fear He might fail you in later years. Not so! That happens, of course, in ordinary life. It happened in the life of David. His best friends had turned against him at the last, and I suppose a lot of people have the same experience; their best friends may turn against them or be unfaithful to them. They do not carry out to the letter what they promised. They disappoint them. It is not as if you have known God for forty or fifty years and that He has never failed you, but then, alas He might fail you. There is no 'might' in it, my friends! There is no possibility of it! That cannot be. It will not be. Therefore trust Him because He is God. 'I am the Lord, I change not' (*Mal. 3:6*).

2. *There are some who trust and are afraid*

And now, as I draw to a close, I want to deal with other characters just for a moment or two. There are some who trust and are afraid. You are perhaps listening to me tonight and you trust in God and yet you are afraid. I have told you before, I think, of an instance in my own experience when I was talking to one of God's real saints, a pious lady who lived near to God. She had communion with God, but she never believed that she was a true Christian. She never had assurance. One day I was sitting with her and I said: 'Look, let us get a Bible'. And we got a Bible and I had it on my knee. I was in no hurry that afternoon, and we were not alone, there was somebody else in the house. I turned to verse after verse, chapter after chapter, and I said, 'Do you believe this?' 'Oh, yes!' She did not deny it. 'Now,' I said at the end, 'if all these things are true of you, and the Bible is true, do you believe the Bible is true?' 'Of course', she said, 'I believe the Bible is true'. 'Well, then,' I said, 'you are a Christian.' 'Oh, yes,' she said, 'but if you knew my heart. . . .' No 'but if' was needed; in that respect she was absolutely wrong. She trusted and she was afraid.

It was the wife of Jonathan Edwards who, on one occasion, convinced by her husband's preaching that she should seek assurance, decided that she would go aside and get this assurance. And she did. She speaks about the flood of light and the fulness of joy that filled her heart when she trusted and lost her fears. She trusted in Him to banish her fear and she knew that she was a child of God, not by her own worthiness, but by her union with the Lord Jesus Christ. I plead with you, my friend, if you trust God tonight, do not be afraid. You say, 'I wish I could get assurance'. Well, if you trust God then you are bound to get it sooner or later. If you trust God then you have assurance, you ought to have assurance, and it is wrong for you not to be assured.

3. *There are some who are afraid, but they do not trust*

For them I am terribly sorry. They are afraid of death; they are afraid of old age and its concomitants; they are afraid of the

Judgment seat and have been afraid for a long time. They are never happy. It does not matter what they get or how they get on; there is always something missing, there is always something lacking, there is always a stone in the shoe – the future, death, the Judgment seat. They are afraid. Year follows year, but they do not trust. O my friends in this sad plight, I am sorry for you! I wish you would get over it. I wish you would trust. I wish you would trust, even now. Why be afraid? Why not get away from all this fear by trusting God? Trusting will solve your problems. You are afraid. You come to church and you do not get what you want, although you have everything that the world can afford to give you. But there is something wrong. You are afraid, but still you do not trust. O my dear friends – you who come here morning and evening, regularly and faithfully, every Sabbath, and who feel that you lack God's blessing and come short of His salvation – I plead with you, seek His face, trust His grace, find deliverance from fear in the work of His dear Son. Trust and bid your fears depart.

4. And last of all, there are some who do not trust and yet they are not afraid

There are some people, no doubt, listening to me tonight and they are as hard as the rocks. They do not fear God and they do not trust God. Nothing makes them afraid. If we speak to them of the fires of hell, and of a lost eternity, and of being with the devil for ever and ever and ever, nothing seems to move them. They put no trust in God for life or for death. They are not afraid of God. I say to all such persons. What a state you are in! What a state you are in! One day you *will* fear, and you will not be able to trust. You will be afraid, but there will be no room for trusting, if you continue in your present state. Cry therefore to the Lord for His mercy and His grace through Christ Jesus!

But just as a parting word I say to God's people, who trust Him by His grace: Trust Him always and in all circumstances. Trust will banish your fears and you will enjoy the happiness of a child of God. You will receive a joy unspeakable and full of glory and at the end you will say when you see death coming near: 'There is laid up for me a crown of righteousness, which the Lord shall give me at that day: and not to me only, but unto all them also that love his appearing' (*2 Tim. 4:8*).

❧ 4 ❧

Receiving of Christ's Fulness

And of his fulness have all we received, and grace for grace.
John 1.16[1]

There has been some doubt as to who spoke these words. Some say
that they were spoken by John the Baptist; others say that they
were written by John the Apostle who wrote the Fourth Gospel. It
does not really matter who spoke them, but what does matter is
that it is true of every believer that he receives of Christ's fulness,
and grace for grace. Clearly, this is not true of everyone. Many
have heard of Christ who never received Him in His fulness. And
some of you here present who hear of His fulness, and who shall
hear a little more of His fulness as I preach to you, continue
deliberately to refuse Him. Is not that sad news? What good will it
do you to have food if you do not eat it, and if your food is set before
you on the table and you are told that you will die if you do not take
it? It is a sad thing indeed if you deliberately refuse it. Every
unbeliever is a lost soul and the only thing that can save him is the
fulness of grace that is in Jesus Christ. Will you yet refuse that
fulness as you hear of it once again? Remember that it is not
enough to come to church. It is not enough to hear the gospel
preached. Some heard it preached and it did not profit them,
because it was not mixed with faith in them who heard it. With
these few words of introduction, and as I put the responsibility
squarely upon your shoulders, I will proceed to the words that we
have in the text.

A person who can truly apply the words of my text to himself has
the fear of God in him. Imagine what it is for a soul to be able to
say, 'I have received out of the fulness of Christ'! What a

[1]February 2, 1975.

[31]

marvellous thing that is for anyone to experience, 'I have received out of the fulness of Christ'! I shall divide the text into three sections: first of all, let us think of it as it describes or reveals a provision; secondly, let us consider it as it relates to Christian experience; and last of all, let us think of it as it gives an assurance concerning the future.

I CHRIST'S FULNESS REVEALS A PROVISION

It is Christ's fulness that we are now talking about. There is – and some would regard this as deep theology – an essential fulness of Christ out of which nobody receives; it is not communicated to any creature, nor can it be. That is the fulness of the Deity. Christ is God. And this fulness that is in Him is an uncreated, infinite fulness, and no creature can possibly receive of it. But our text does not refer to the fulness that Christ has as God, or to the fulness that He had from all eternity as God. Clearly it refers to a fulness that is in Christ and which can be communicated by Christ because He became incarnate.

The fulness of Christ as our Saviour and Mediator is a different fulness from His fulness as purely and absolutely God. When Christ became incarnate He became man but He did not cease to be God. He was God and man. He became man; He never became God. He always was God but He was not always man. If it is possible to speak of one miracle surpassing another, there is no miracle greater than the incarnation of Jesus Christ. It is not nearly as great a miracle that Jesus dies on the cross as that Jesus, the eternal Son of God, was in a virgin's womb. It is not nearly as great a miracle that He rose from the dead as that He, who is the eternal God became the same kind of person, the same kind of man, as you and I are, but without sin. We are dust; and He became dust. You must never think that the body of Christ was of a higher calibre or of a higher nature than your body; it was not. You are dust and to dust you will return. Christ also returned to the dust; He died, His body was capable of dying. He could die only because He had the kind of body that you and I have. He became man in order that He might by His own doing communicate to us of the fulness of His grace, and enrich us by doing so. And His entire work on our behalf was the result of His marvellous love. But at this point I must tell you briefly what the text before us does not mean.

It is a terrible thing to twist and pervert the gospel; it is just as terrible to remove the essence of the gospel. If you received a sugar-coated tablet from the doctor for your health and you ate the sugar coat but threw away the tablet, what good would the tablet do you? The healing property of the tablet is not found in the sugar coating but in what is underneath. Similarly, when the Apostle says, 'Out of His fulness have all we received', this does not mean that we have received a form of moral behaviour through the example of Jesus Christ. Many people teach that Christ died in order to show us the qualities which He Himself had and so make us holy. For example, we are naturally impatient. Christ was infinitely patient, and these people say, 'Oh, you should be patient as Jesus was patient'. Of course you should, but that is not what the Bible means by holiness. He did not die in order to show us patience. He did not become incarnate merely for this. My text does not carry that meaning yet the error is often taught, that if you are this and if you are that, 'the same as Jesus was – gentle, meek, mild, temperate, patient,' and so on, then you possess holiness. But holiness does not begin there at all. Christ did not become incarnate, neither did He die, merely to show these qualities to us.

What then did Christ come to earth to do? In other words, what is the true meaning of my text? You will find the key to it in the verse following the text: 'For the law was given by Moses but grace and truth came by Jesus Christ'. So, here is a contrast made.

Moses is mentioned as the greatest of the Old Testament prophets. The law came by him. Nothing came by Moses but the law. But by Jesus Christ came grace and truth. The law, the moral law, had no grace in it from beginning to end. Its meaning was, do this or you will die. It was given as our schoolmaster to turn us to Christ. The law itself, although it leads us to Christ, has no grace in it; but grace and truth came by Jesus Christ. 'Of his fulness have all we received, and grace for grace'. We must ask what grace we have received out of the fulness of Christ, God's only begotten Son who became incarnate, and lived on earth and died, and rose again the third day according to the Scriptures. What grace, then, have all we received?

II CHRIST'S FULNESS AND CHRISTIAN EXPERIENCE

1. First of all, there is the grace of forgiveness

It was to give us this that Jesus came. He became incarnate to communicate forgiveness to the guilty sinner. And this is what John means when he says, Of His fulness have we, as guilty creatures, received, the grace of forgiveness. And what a great thing that is when we look at it in the light of the sinner's guilt! The magnitude of sin no one can declare, but the magnitude of forgiveness is greater than the magnitude of sin. And we have received out of His fulness that which covers all our sins, mercy to cover them all. There is no adequate illustration of it. The prophet Micah speaks of God casting all the sins of believers into the depths of the sea. As the ocean covers all things in its depths so are our sins covered by Jesus Christ. I may even say that our sins are annihilated, they are as if they had not had being, as if they had been blotted out of existence. God remembers them against His people no more. And all by the grace of God! We have received grace for grace. Grace has taken away all our sins. Oh, my friends, what marvellous grace we have received out of His goodness! But, of course, you could never receive this, except out of His fulness. If you compare this with the forgiveness that man may give you, what is that? It is nothing at all, however rich and noble and magnanimous it may be. It is nothing at all in comparison with the grace that, out of God's fulness, we sinners have received, grace to annihilate sin, to put it out of existence for ever and ever.

2. Then, too, there is the grace of justification

There has been a newspaper notice recently concerning a woman who was found guilty of taking away life unlawfully but set free by the Court of Appeal. It had been found that the judge had erred in his summing up to the jury and on that technical point of law she was freed. Now that freedom does not justify anybody from guilt; that is not justification. If the Court of Appeal had found that this woman had not committed the offence of which she had been declared guilty, then she would have been justified, but it was not so; she was only freed on a technical point of law. She was not justified, she was only freed. There have been people, in history

[34]

records, who have been accused of crimes against the state, and I refer particularly to the case in French history where a commissioned officer in the army – his name was Dreyfus – was accused of betraying his country. After several years the Republic of France offered him a pardon, but he would not take it. He said that he did not want a pardon. He claimed that there was nothing which he should be pardoned for, he had never committed the crime of which he was accused. What he wanted was justification and ultimately after many years, the case was re-tried and it was found to the satisfaction of the nation that the man had been falsely accused. When this was found out he was justified and freed. He had never committed any offence. But our own case is quite different from that of Dreyfus. We are guilty of crimes against God. What by any stretch of the imagination can justify us? How can we be justified after committing sins without number? Only by the person and work of Christ who was made sin for us, made a curse for us, that we might be made the righteousness of God in Him (*2 Cor. 5:21*). Christ obeyed God's law on behalf of believers; He took their sins also in His own body to the tree. It is in this way that God remains just and becomes the justifier of sinners who by grace believe in His dear Son. And when God Himself justifies His elect, 'Who is he that condemneth'?

I suppose some people discuss among themselves the question, 'Are the sins which the believer commits between his conversion and his death forgiven him? Is he justified from them?' In other words, is he justified even in respect of sins not yet committed? To my mind that is not a question worthy of much discussion. It would be a slur on the completeness of the grace of God to give the answer 'No' to this question. According to Scripture, when the believer is justified, he is not only justified from all sins committed by him before he became a believer, and from original sin also, but he is justified for ever and ever. He is justified from sins past, present, and future. His justification is utterly complete and final. But I hasten to add that this will not give rise *to* sin; nor give us licence to sin. It will be our prayer *not* to sin.

3. Furthermore, out of Christ's fulness believers receive the grace of love

In marvellous grace believers are married unto Jesus Christ. It is written in Isaiah's prophecy, 'Thy maker is thine husband'. And again, there is the grace of comfort. This will cause our fears to vanish. There is also the grace of holiness, by which we are made like unto Himself, the grace of being purified. I have only touched upon the fringe of these various graces. Let me urge you to search them out in your Bibles.

III CHRIST'S FULNESS AND ASSURANCE FOR THE FUTURE

Christ's fulness is an unfathomable fulness. I shall not attempt to give you illustrations, because there are no illustrations that I can use that will give an adequate idea of what this 'fulness' means. The Apostle Paul uses the phrase, 'the unsearchable riches of Christ', and he clearly means the unfathomableness, the unsearchableness, of the grace that is in Jesus Christ. In the last two or three years, men have discovered more of the vastness of the universe. Years ago they thought that the stars were quite small things, points of light somewhere in the sky, and quite near to the earth; now they have discovered the tremendous vastness of the universe. Men have even reached the moon and have measured the distances between the earth and certain stars in billions of light years. But my point is that the universe is not unsearchable. We lack the means of seeing beyond what we now see. Men do not possess telescopes powerful enough to reach out beyond our present knowledge, but, and I repeat the point, the universe is *not* unsearchable. What makes the universe unsearchable is our inadequacy of knowledge, our incapacity and our limitation. But that is not what makes the grace of God unsearchable. What makes the grace of God unsearchable is that it is infinite in itself. It cannot be fully searched because it is the fulness of the Deity, the fulness of the uncreated, infinite God.

And yet again, Christ's fulness is an inexhaustible fulness. It does not matter how many have already received of it, it is inexhaustible. It is not like the flood in the time of Noah. It rained for forty days and forty nights and the waters roared and covered the tops of the mountains. But the deluge subsided and the ground became dry again. If I may be pardoned for using the illustration, what you have in our text is the rain of the divine fulness. It never ceases to pour, and therefore the waters never cease. It is inexhaustible. There is no waste involved in it, there is no end to it, because it is the fulness of the Godhead. There was an end to the storehouses of Joseph in Egypt; there was plenty for all even for outsiders like Jacob's sons; plenty for years of famine; but after all there was a limit to it. But there is no limit to God's fulness. There was a limit to the riches of Boaz as contrasted with the poverty of Ruth. But there is no limit to the riches of Jesus Christ, although sometimes unbelief makes us think there is.

But I must pause here to sound a note of warning not only to those of you who are not Christians, but also to those who desire a word of encouragement. If you are not a Christian and afraid that your sins are too many, or too heinous, too evil, for the grace of God to cover you and to forgive you, then you are limiting God. You cannot be guilty of a greater sin than that of unbelief. As God's servant I must warn you against it. It does not matter what your sins are; it does not matter how many they are; out of God's fulness you may receive grace for grace, grace to cover all your sins. Never let unbelief linger in your mind for it is dishonouring to God. But some people say, 'Oh, I wish I hadn't committed that sin; if I had not done so there would be some hope for me'. I tell you plainly, that that thought comes from the devil. The Scripture tells us that God's grace can cover all sins.

Next, a word to the believer. You are anxious sometimes; you are afraid. You are afraid of what may happen to you. You are full of fear about your circumstances. Now listen! 'Of his fulness have all we received, and grace for grace'. Do you mean to say that you are afraid that some problem will come your way that will be so big that it cannot be met and overcome by the grace of God! I am sorry to tell you that sometimes I think along this same line. We are poor people in this sinful world, and we ourselves are sinful. Unbelief sometimes gets the better of us. There are times when we give way and are afraid. But I am not saying this to encourage anyone to give way to it. It is most dishonouring to God when you and I think that anything will ever come our way for which there is not sufficient grace in God to lift us up.

When Spurgeon went as a young man to preach in London and there were thousands listening to him night and day, he was little more than a lad. One day as he was walking in the city he began to say to himself: 'I might as well give up; I just cannot continue facing this tremendous crowd; I shall not have enough to give them; I shall run out of texts and out of preaching matter'. He was very much depressed over it all but then he said, 'I imagined myself to be like a wee fish in the sea fearing, "there will not be enough for me to drink"'. 'A wee fish in the sea!' He was an Englishman, so he would not have used the word 'wee'! Probably he said, 'a little fish'. Imagine a little fish saying, 'I am afraid the ocean will dry up and there will not be enough for me to drink'. And, he added, 'I saw myself, and my own folly, and I laughed and laughed at my own folly'. Can you imagine it! But there is another thing. Think of the small haddock in the sea, perhaps in the vastness of the Atlantic Ocean, thinking within itself, 'I am afraid there will not be room enough here in this ocean for me. I fear the day will come when I shall have no room to move'. Imagine the blackbird or the robin saying, 'I am afraid that very soon there will not be room enough in the universe for me. It is possible to fly just now from branch to branch, but I fear that the space will get so narrow, or that I shall become so big, that there will not be room for me'. How foolish that would be! But it is not nearly as foolish as it is on the part of Christian men or women to say that they fear they will come into circumstances where there will not be a sufficiency of the fulness of the grace of God to meet their need. The truth is, that when God gives out of His fulness the fulness that is in Him never grows less. 'Of his *fulness* have all we received'. God has given, God gives, God continues to give, and He shall do so for ever and ever.

It is important for us to realize that as we receive 'grace for grace', the very act of receiving creates within us an experience of immense value. Let me explain. First of all, the day when you received of His fulness was a day when you were absolutely conscious of your own emptiness. You cannot fill what is not empty. A tank must be empty before you can fill it. Ah, but you say, there could be a little at the bottom of it. Perhaps, in the way we often talk, that is true, but it is not what our text means. It means that when you came to the Cross you came with an empty vessel, absolutely empty of your own righteousness, and of your own good works. You used to depend upon your morality and upon your innocence but God emptied you. And if you are ever going to be filled with the fulness of Christ again – and you ought to be every day of your life – you will never be filled with His fulness unless and until you are absolutely empty. Sometimes people say to me: 'I really have nothing'. I reply: 'I am glad to hear it'. If people have nothing, then they are ready for Christ to fill them; if they are really empty, then they are in the best state for Christ to fill them.

Look at the matter in this way. When we are unwell and visit the doctor, it is usually one or two things that are wrong with us. Nobody goes to the doctor when everything is wrong with them. But supposing there was a doctor who would never look at you until everything was wrong with you. Perhaps you can hardly suppose that; but that is the way in which we as sinners come to Christ. Everything is wrong with us. We have no help, we have no soundness; but then, out of His fulness we receive grace for grace. It is a good thing to feel empty, if it sends you to the right place. But it is not a sign of the soul's health for people to say they are empty one week, and then, when you go to see them the next week, you find they are just as empty as they were earlier; and then they are as empty the next month also. They ought to be filled out of the Lord's fulness. But as I have already said, the more they are filled, the more they see their own emptiness.

There must be a voluntary acceptance of the fulness of Christ received by faith. God does not come, as it were, and force this on you. He does not throw it into your heart against your will. Do not misunderstand me. There is no conflict involved here. When you receive out of His fulness you receive it with all your heart and soul and mind and strength. You receive it because you see its sufficiency, its glory, its fulness and its freeness. You see its suitableness for you and this makes you receive it into your heart. You say, 'this fulness is the very thing for me; it is enough for me'. It is given to you for nothing, and if you receive it, you receive all that your Lord can give you. Sometimes you may receive it with a trembling hand; the hand that takes it may be weak. I compare it to the case of people who have Parkinson's disease; they get shaky if you give them a cup of tea; you can only half-fill the cup, because they will spill it. Similarly, sometimes we are so weak in faith that our hands tremble, as if we had a spiritual disease. But even then, although faith is rather weak and you can take only one mouthful of the fulness of His grace, you will be strengthened more and more to drink richly and to your own enjoyment.

Oh what satisfaction, what marvellous satisfaction, when you receive it, as did the Ethiopian eunuch who went on his way rejoicing! You must take of the Lord's fulness frequently – daily, hourly it ought to be. Why do you not receive it more often? When did you last drink out of the fulness of Christ Jesus? The question applies to me too. Do not think that I am putting the question to you alone. When did I stoop down low enough to drink from this river of water of life that flows from the throne of God and of the Lamb?

There are two things that I want to press upon you, before I conclude. First of all, I want to say to every believer here listening to me: Trust the Lord Jesus Christ, trust in His fulness; it is there for you. And it is richer than anything I can describe. Trust Him then. Never fail in your faith. Trust Him, and although you do not receive Him as much as you would like to do, you will always receive as much as you need. And in a day to come you will receive far more than you receive now. There is another world to which we are going.

> *The streams on earth I've tasted,*
> *More deep I'll drink above.*
> *There, to an ocean fulness,*
> *His mercy doth expand,*
> *And glory, glory dwelleth*
> *In Immanuel's land.*

And one day we shall be saturated and soaked, for ever immersed in the fulness that is in Christ Jesus. But that is reserved for heaven; it is not for this world. You will never receive as much as you would like in this world, but you will always get, as I said, as much as you require.

My second word in closing is to the unconverted, and it is simply this: do not refuse the fulness that is in Christ Jesus for your soul. There is nothing else that can save you. Even though you could get all the gold and silver in the world, it would not take away one of your sins. Whatever you do, do not refuse Christ's fulness of grace. Are you refusing it? Why are you refusing it? If you continue to refuse it, you will go to hell and whatever else there is there, there is not a drop of God's fulness of grace, not a drop! Will you not take it now while it is offered to you without money and without price?

∽ 5 ∽

Sins Forgiven

O Israel, thou shalt not be forgotten of me. I have blotted out, as a thick cloud, thy transgressions, and, as a cloud, thy sins; return unto me; for I have redeemed thee.

Isaiah 44:21–22[1]

There are two observations that I would like to make by way of introduction. The first of them is, that unless we take our place in the presence of God as needy and lost sinners, the gospel and the preaching of the gospel will be of no use to us whatsoever. That is an obvious truth. The primary fault of the Pharisees and of the majority of the Jews in the days of Christ was that they refused to take the place of sinners. Unbelief debarred them from blessing. Now it is equally true of us that, in every sermon, if we are not conscious of our need, and if we are not expectant that the sermon might lead us to Christ, our healer and Saviour, the sermon will not do us any good. God has no room for the self-sufficient at the throne of grace, and at the throne of mercy. He came, not to call the righteous, but sinners to repentance. Now that is the first observation, and I hope it will sink into all hearts here present.

The second observation is that we cannot be but astounded at the longsuffering of God. We see it in this chapter of Isaiah, where He makes a mockery of those people who made gods for themselves. A man plants a tree and he sees it grow. Then he cuts it down and takes part of it and makes firewood of it. He bakes his bread with it and he roasts his flesh with it – then he cuts another part of it and he gives it to the joiner who makes the figure of a man. He then falls down before this part of the tree that he himself has planted and seen growing, and he says to it, 'Thou art my God'. It

---

[1]Preached at a Communion at Dingwall.

is amazing how longsuffering God is towards people who spurn His offer of grace year after year. We see it in our chapter where God says: 'Remember these, O Jacob and Israel; for thou art my servant: I have formed thee. . . . I have blotted out, as a thick cloud, thy transgressions, and, as a cloud, thy sins: return unto me, for I have redeemed thee.'

We find the same truth expressed in an equally graphic way in the prophecy of Jeremiah where the nation of Israel is likened to a treacherous and unfaithful wife. She was married but she proved unfaithful to her husband; she went after other men. Now obviously that breaks the marriage connection between a man and woman. And after this has happened, not once nor twice, but after it has happened over the centuries, the Lord says, 'Turn unto me, for I am married unto you, O backsliding children' (*Jer. 3:14*). My friends, it is a marvel of grace that the infidelity of these people did not break their marriage union with God, the covenant union with which He favoured them. And it is equally a marvel of grace that there are some of you here tonight, who have heard the gospel more often than you can remember but you have refused to believe. And yet tonight, once again, God has given you the privilege of coming to Him, as if he had said, 'What more could I have done to my vineyard that I have not done?' (*Isa. 5:4*). How longsuffering God is! For He could cut you down as an unfruitful tree that cumbers the ground. Here, then, we have an example of the superabundance of the mercy of God.

Now there are three thoughts in the words themselves to which I want to draw your attention, as simply as I can. First of all, we see how our sins are described; they are described as 'a thick cloud'. Secondly, we see how our sins are blotted out. Thirdly, we see how sin affects our lives.

I SINS DESCRIBED

How our sins are described

They are described here as 'a thick cloud'. We know the origin of the clouds; we know that they do not come from above, they come from below. They rise up from the earth and from the ocean; this is the way the clouds form. We also know the plain fact about sin, and I think it is quite legitimate to say that sin comes from below. We do not know the origin – nobody will ever know the origin – but we know how sin came into the world. Man was innocent and the devil came and tempted him and then he sinned. How sin came to be at first, nobody knows and nobody will ever know, unless it be revealed by God to His own people. It remains a mystery, but we do know that it comes from below. Jesus put the Jews right on this very question when they mentioned something about the washing of hands before taking food at meals. Jesus did not speak of the unhygienic but He said to them regarding their sin, 'This does not make a man any more sinful than if he did not wash his hands'. He told them that they ought to know that defilement does not come from without to within, but that it comes from within to without; and then He said: 'Out of the heart proceed evil thoughts, murders, adulteries, fornications, thefts, false witness, blasphemies' (*Matt. 15:18–20*). He gave a catalogue of sins of which people are guilty in this world. And He said that the heart of man is the fountain; it is but the streams that you see. Every sin has its source in the heart. This is the fountain-head from which sin flows.

Sin is in the heart of us all; indeed, all sin is in the heart of us all. And if we try to make out that we are better in our hearts than others are, we are only deceiving ourselves. We may be better in our lives than others are. Thank God we have lives different from those of many people, but we have not different hearts. The same kind of heart we all have, out of which come all these things. But there is another thought here, which perhaps it would be profitable to mention. It is this: there are some thoughts which do not originate in the heart but which are put in it by the devil direct. Certain things rise in our hearts, but they do not belong to us, sinners though we are. Some may be thoughts of blasphemy, thoughts that you would not think a human being could possibly conceive. Now, friends, I maintain that, evil as we are, these thoughts do not rise from ourselves direct, they are instilled into us by the direct and mysterious agency of the devil and it is he who does it. And I know that this is, in a measure, a comfort to me and it ought to be a comfort to you. Not that I am comforted by the fact that sin is in me. Far from it! But I am comforted by the fact that certain temptations do not rise from inside us.

Sometime ago I had a letter from an old friend of mine in Lewis who has since gone to glory. He was telling me about the conversion of his own son who did not live very long after it. The son told his father that vile thoughts rose up in his heart as he lay there on his bed, but he also said to his father – and he was only a young Christian – 'I know that they don't come from myself, they must come from the father of lies, from Satan'. I believe he was quite right. Now this is by way of comfort, but they are our sins all the same. Though they come from without in that way, if we give them any welcome, if we harbour them in any way, if we do not plead before God and resist them, they will become our sins, although they did not originate with us.

One effect of the clouds is that they obstruct our view of sun. When we live in a dark day, the clouds overhang us; we do not see the sun; the sun is there, of course, as usual, but we do not see it. We do not feel its warmth, we do not get its light, as we would normally do on a bright, cloudless day. And this is what sin does. Sin blinds the eye of the soul, and of the mind, to the beauty of Christ. My friends, this is the reason why you, who desire to see His beauty, do not see it. Sin blinds your eye; there is a veil of darkness; clouds of transgression come between you and your Saviour. If they were removed you would see His glory as 'the glory as of the only begotten of the Father, full of grace and truth' (*John 1:14*). There are many of you here tonight, and Christ is not fair in your eyes. You do not love Him, you do not have any fellowship with Him, you do not hold communion with Him. He means nothing to you. He is despised and rejected by you.

Do you know why you despise and reject Him? You will not venture to say that it is anything that is wrong within your own hearts; you will not venture to say that He is not the glory of the heavens above, the Father's delight and the adoration of the angels. You will not venture to say these things. Why, then, do you not see His beauty? It is because there is this veil of transgression; there are these clouds of sin between you and Him. They hide from you the glory of the Lord Jesus Christ. You cannot love sin and love Christ at the same time. You fail to see the greatness and the goodness of God, if this cloud is above you, if this cloud is upon your soul and in your mind, this blindness, as the Scripture calls it. You cannot see Him. Nor can you see Christ and His glory in others, that is to say, in His people. There are those of you who see the Lord's people round about you, and if you cannot find

[44]

anything else to criticize your criticize them. And even when you cannot find any true cause for which to criticize them, you find fault with them instead, and say they are hypocrites and you speak all manner of evil against them falsely. Why is this? I am not saying that the Lord's people are perfect. It is not so. But it is because of this mist of sin, this blackness of evil that is over your minds, that you fault-finders fail to see the image of Christ in the poorest of His flock. Failing to see the beauty of Christ, you also fail to see His beauty in His people. And you turn what ought to be a midday of grace into a midnight of sin.

In the Scriptures, clouds sometimes represent the evil of sin, the evils that are consequent upon sin, tribulation and punishment and wrath. These clouds not only hide the sunlight, but sometimes they come down as showers, issuing from the clouds, perhaps not always light showers but sometimes as drenching storms. Sometimes the evils that are in the clouds of transgression come down upon the consciences of many, at least when they are young. They come down upon their consciences as showers, as it were, of what the anger of God really is. Have you ever lived for five minutes under the misery of the displeasure of God in your conscience? If you have done so, you have tasted what hell is like. It is hell to be conscious of the displeasure of God against you. Sometimes these clouds come down, as it were, in great heavy drops into your conscience and into your mind and you know what an evil thing sin can be. You learn that it involves tribulation and punishment and wrath.

The Scripture speaks of clouds of transgressions, representing sins that cannot be numbered. Clouds are formed of innumerable particles and who can ever measure sin? The Psalmist said, concerning his own sins, that they were more than he could reckon, more than the hairs upon his head. There is a sense in which we can say that sin is an infinite evil. I tell you, there are innumerably more sins in you than you ever thought there were. Perhaps you think only of one or two sins that you have committed, sins that have seemed outstanding in your life, and you wish more than anything that you had not committed them. My friends, terrible though that may be, it is not nearly as terrible in the sight of God as the innumerable sins of which you are not even conscious. Such is the subtlety of sin that it hides its expansiveness from you. Widespread as it is, going into every fibre of your being, yet you do not see it.

And then there is the enormity of sin. The Lord calls it 'a *thick* cloud'. It is so enormous that you cannot measure it by its punishment. You cannot measure sin even by its endless punishment in the place where time is no more. You cannot measure it by hell, where the devils are, and where they are to be chained for ever. Not even by these things can you measure the enormity of sin. There is only one place where you can measure it, and that is on the cross of Calvary, if you have any understanding of that cross. There you see in history, as is revealed in the Bible, the Son of God hanging between earth and heaven, and crying out, 'My God, my God, why hast thou forsaken me?' That, my friend, is the measure of sin. Now you cannot understand that! Nobody can understand what it involved for God the Father to forsake God the Son, and what it involved for God the Son, the incarnate Son upon the cross, to be abandoned, forsaken by God the Father for sin. Nobody can understand it. But if you are hoping to understand the enormity of sin, that is the place where you can get an idea of it – not in the punishment of sinful men in time or eternity but in the sufferings of the incarnate Son of God at Calvary.

Again clouds usually cause darkness and coldness and joylessness. If it is a cloudy day, if you have a day to spend by yourself, you wish it were brighter; you wish the clouds would vanish, so that you would enjoy the day. Clouds keep away the warmth of the sun. Similarly, no life that is under the cloud of transgression can cultivate joy. I am not saying that there is not joy in sin, in revellings and suchlike. I am not saying that there is no pleasure in adultery and fornication and in uncleanness and covetousness. I am not saying that. That would be wrong. 'Stolen waters are sweet', says the Bible (*Prov. 9:17*). Yes, of course, there is joy in them, and yet it brings its own misery in the end. Once you sin against your God, you are never the same again. You are the same person but there is, as it were, a shadow following you for the rest of your life. A darkness comes over you that you never get rid of, once you have sinned against God. It takes away the joy, it takes away everything you ought to be.

God made you to glorify Him. He made you to enjoy Him, and not only in the world to come. The Shorter Catechism begins by telling us God created man to glorify Him and enjoy Him forever. It does not mean that man is to glorify Him in the world to come only, but to glorify Him in this world and in the world to come, and to enjoy Him in this world and in the world to come. You are meant to enjoy God and God did everything in the redemptive plan to make you happy. God did not put a restrictive prohibition or a restrictive thing in the moral law except with your welfare and your happiness in mind. Everything God prohibits you from doing contributes to making you happy. Everything He commands you to do is to make you happy. How then can you say that God's opposition to sin in your life leaves you joyless and cold? It is not pleasant to have to speak about sin and sins, but I hope that by the grace of God, you have been convinced of what this thing is in your heart. If so, let us now go on to the next thing we need to consider.

II SIN BLOTTED OUT

The wonderful thing is that God blots out sin as a thick cloud. I repeat it; this is indeed wonderful news. It is almost unbelievable news, but the Bible leaves us in no doubt about it. Let us look into it together.

First of all, we are taught the helplessless of man. What does God say? 'I have blotted out as a thick cloud thy sins.' You have your cloudy days and you wish the clouds were taken away. But can you take them away? No, you cannot do so any more than you can create them. You can do nothing about them. You have to wait until they go away, for you have no power whatsoever over them, none at all. Even in our age of scientific wonders, to move the clouds cannot be done. The clouds come and the clouds go, but man has no control over them to discipline them. The same thing is true about sins. Do you try to remove your own sins? Are they like a load upon your conscience? Are they like darkness upon your mind? You say, 'I try my best to remove them'. God knows how many ways people invent to remove them. They try their best. They may go and pray about them. Well, you might as well not go. Do not misunderstand me. I am not depreciating the fact of your prayers. I am not telling people not to pray. But if you think that your prayers can abolish your sin, can dissipate your sins, can annihilate your sins, you are only adding to the thick cloud. You try it and see, and you will know that I am right. When these sins come upon you and you go and pray about them, I hope to God you do not feel better just because you prayed about your sins. Your sins are still there and your prayer cannot move them. No, they are too high for you, far too high, you cannot reach them. They are too enormous for you, they are too heavy for you, they are too thick for you, they are too many for you.

Let me change the figure. You can think of sin as a debt, a debt that cannot be remitted by the efforts of man. But God says that *He* will blot them out. And this is the news that I should like to give you. God says, '*I*' – note this word of just one letter – '*I* have blotted out, as a thick cloud, thy transgressions, and as a cloud thy sins: return unto me for *I* have redeemed thee'. This is what God says: '*I*' have done this. I would like to ring the changes in that one word. What does it mean? It means that everything that God is, is summed up in this one little pronoun 'I'. He is One who delights to say: 'I have done it in mercy, I have done it in justice, I have done it in compassion, and I have done it in love – I have done it. I have blotted them out, not for your sake but for my own sake; I have done it, with the power of my right hand. I have done it in righteousness, I have done it in truth, I have done it in love, I have done it in mercy.' For His own name's sake He has done it.

You can look upon everything that God did as recorded in Scripture, from the first promise of a coming Redeemer, the 'seed of the woman', right on to the redeeming work of Jesus Christ when He died on the cross. And this is what it means: 'I have blotted out as a thick cloud thy sins, I have done it'. Oh, the right hand of God, my friends, the hand of mercy! I could go on to say how justice could have prevented mercy, but then God found out a way in His own infinite wisdom by which the work of salvation could be done justly. And the flood-gates were open for mercy and compassion. The love of God came like a deluge upon the children of men. Sins were carried away – 'blotted out' – and when you looked up into the sky there was not a cloud remaining. What a wonderful experience that is!

Have you ever seen a man bowed down to the earth? You cannot speak to him. No man can be more miserable than he is. Why? Because of his sin. I remember a man, an old man, and if ever there was a religious man, it was he. He was religious from his youth up; then he married and brought up a family and he lived to see his grandchildren. He was exceptionally good to the cause of Christ. He did not belong to my congregation, that is to say, to the first congregation I had. I was a long time in my present one before he came to me. By this time he was an old man, well over eighty, and he was religious, as religious as one could be. He never missed a prayer meeting; he always read the Bible. He seemed to be everything that a man could be. And then he became convinced that he was a lost sinner. One day he came to the manse and I tried to comfort him. I tried to tell him about Muckle Kate of Lochcarron who lost her eyesight, weeping for her sins; but he would not listen to me. When I told him about her, he said, 'All her misery was nothing compared to mine; there was never anybody like me; there cannot be anybody like I am'. And he said these things weeping his eyes out all the time. Well, so it was, and what could I do? I could point him to the Scriptures, but it was all of no avail. After a while I went to see him again, and he had something to tell me – I think he had sent for me, if I remember rightly. He told me that he had found Christ, that every cloud had been taken away, and that by the grace of God his sins were taken away, his sins of eighty-five years, his sin of self-righteousness and self-sufficiency. He had been long under a cloud and this is what lay heavy upon his soul; but God had taken it away, and he said, 'I see Christ in His mercy and His love.'

Well, that is what God does. The clouds are thick, and sometimes they empty themselves on us, but God in His mercy takes them away. We read in the Book of Psalms, 'If thou, Lord, shouldest mark iniquities, O Lord, who shall stand? But there is forgiveness with thee, that thou mayest be feared' (*130:3-4*).

Now let me draw your attention to a scene – to a scene that took place historically nearly two thousand years ago. When our Lord, the despised Nazarene, was hanging on a cross and all the clouds of God's fury had emptied themselves upon His innocent head and soul, there was darkness upon the face of the earth – perhaps a merciful darkness, I do not know – perhaps it was to hide from the eyes of all human beings something that was too sacred for them to behold. As Christ hung there in the gloom, every single drop in the cloud of the fury of God against the sins of the elect fell upon His innocent soul – and all in the space of a few hours. Every drop fell upon Him! He cried out in His agony, 'I thirst'. His thirst in dying was caused by the deluge of the wrath of God poured out upon His soul. My friend, this is how God accomplished the work of redemption. He says, 'I have blotted out, as a thick cloud, thy transgressions.' O my friends, remember these words! Remember

Christ, remember the cross and what He suffered! Do not think of His physical sufferings only, but remember what God did to Him, He poured upon Him *all* His wrath against the sins of His elect. 'All we like sheep have gone astray, we have turned everyone to his own way, and the Lord hath laid on Him the iniquity of us all.' You have everything in that text (*Isa. 53:6*).

A minister was once about to board a train when a man came to him and said, 'You are a minister?' and he replied, 'Yes'. The man went on, 'I am a lost sinner, I wish you could direct me to Christ.' The minister looked at his watch and said to him, 'Only two minutes remain before the departure of the train. He told him to go home and read Isaiah, chapter 53. The man went home and turned to his Bible and this is what he read, 'All we like sheep have gone astray, we have turned every one to his own way, and the Lord hath laid on him the iniquity of us all.' And that is how he got the meaning of the gospel.

There is so much more to say. When the clouds are taken away, then the warmth of God's love comes into your soul. How I would like to dwell upon that – the warmth of God's love coming into the soul. My friends, there is no experience outside heaven like it. You feel that the clouds of God's wrath are going to come down upon your head, and then, all of a sudden, they vanish away and the sun of His countenance shines on you with all its sweetness and love and warmth. It is heaven to the soul, at least it is like heaven, and it will lead to heaven. You know how Jesus said to a certain man: 'Thy sins are forgiven thee' – 'There is now no more condemnation for thee. I look upon thee with favour. I love thee, thou art my child!' What warmth comes into the soul! 'I have blotted out, I have blotted out completely – *completely* – every one of your sins'. This is what it means – I have blotted them all out.

'Ah,' but you say, 'my sins are not all blotted out. If you only knew how many a day and how many a night I look up to heaven to the One who, I hope, is my Father, and I cannot see His face, because of the clouds that are between me and Jesus! I want to see Jesus, my Saviour, and I cannot see Him because of these thick clouds that are between me and Him.' Listen, my friend, you are looking for comfort in your feelings, instead of looking to the Saviour Himself by faith. He said 'I *have* blotted out your sins'; they are not there anymore; God has taken them away. You only think they are there, because of your consciousness of them. It is a good thing for you to have a broken and a contrite heart in order that you may seek His grace more and more, but I assure you again that the sins of believers are not laid to their charge any more.

There is an expression in the Bible that is very remarkable indeed. It is used of the Deity. We find it in Isaiah 43:25: 'I, even I, am he that blotteth out thy transgressions for mine own sake, and *will not remember thy sins*'. Again, we find that this promise of God not to remember His people's sins belongs to the covenant of grace as we find it expressed in Jeremiah 31:33, 34: 'I will forgive their iniquity and I will remember their sin no more'. We rejoice in this; we know that God sees everything in the past and in the present; we are sure that all things are open and naked before Him; and yet we are equally sure that God, in the exercise of His grace, will not remember our sins, but cast them behind His back, as we read happened in the case of King Hezekiah (*Isa. 38:17*). How He does it we do not know, and we do not want to know. The Psalmist knew much when he asked God to forgive him. There are sins of the body, sins of the eye, sins of the ear. Many a time your tongue and your hand and your feet sin. There are sins of the mind, thoughts, imagination; sins against life, sins in your home, repeated sins, presumptuous sins, doubting, backsliding, blasphemy; sins against God the Father directly, against God the Son directly; sins against the Holy Spirit, quenching, striving, resisting Him. And yet says God to His people, 'I have blotted them *all* out.' Oh, what an expanse of mercy there is in God! What a universe of mercy, what boundless mercies, what heavenly mercies, what eternal mercies, divine mercies! 'I have blotted all your sins out,' says the Lord. Only His power could do that. You cannot blot them out from your own memory and perhaps you cannot blot out some of your sins from your character. You may be one of those unfortunate people who has fallen into open sin some way or other, and I suppose it will follow you all the days of your life. But never mind! Come to Christ and as you do so, though people will remember it against you, God will remember it no more. God has already put it behind His back, if you have believed on His Son. And never mind what people say. And this is the comfort that I want to give you when you remember and when people remember, God says 'I will remember their sin no more'.

III SIN AFFECTING OUR LIVES

I must say a little about how our lives are affected by it all. You cannot have your sins forgiven, you cannot look up into the bright sky and see the face of God by faith, and be the same man or woman that you were before. What happens to you? Well, your soul is filled with adoration and you cry out, 'Blessed be the name of the Lord and praise be unto God for ever and for ever. Unto Him that washed us from our sins in His own blood, be glory, power and dominion, for ever and ever'. You cannot help singing such words as these. Your love is stirred up for the One who has saved and forgiven you. The peace that you have passes all understanding. You cannot but be moved. And at home and at work, indoors and out of doors, you desire to possess that holiness 'without which no man shall see the Lord' (*Heb. 12:14*). You do not want to live the life that you lived before; you do not want to live under the sins of the flesh. Forsaking your sins, you return penitently and lovingly to God.

So this is what God says to you, to you who believe in Jesus. And if you die tonight, if you fall dead, you do not need to be afraid; you do not need to fear; God has blotted out your sins, they are no more. You go to the Judgment seat; your sins will be no more. You have no need to be afraid. And if you live for many years and you think of death, which is sure to come, that does not make you afraid. Death itself may cause you to fear for it is foreign to our nature, but death itself has been conquered by our Lord, and as He Himself entered into glory, He will bring all His people to glory also. He has promised to do it.

But what about those who are not believers? What shall I say to you? I would not be faithful to my office, or to my God, if I did not say to you that dark clouds are hanging over you. They have been hanging over you for thirty, forty, fifty, sixty or more years. You are retired perhaps; you have settled down in this world; but the clouds are hanging over you, and one of these days they are going to break! It will be as when the deluge came upon all men in the time of Noah; they never believed it would come, but one day the fountains of the deep were opened and the rains came down and covered the valleys and the hills and there was no place in which men could find safety. God saved Noah and his family, but all unbelievers perished. My friends, when gospel days are done;

when the sun goes down, and the gospel will not be preached to you any more, then these dark clouds will gather. They will come down upon you, and they will weigh your soul down to all eternity in a place where there is no mercy. Are you not afraid of that? Well, be afraid, and come now in repentance and faith to the only Saviour of sinners, who alone is able to blot out as a thick cloud your transgressions and as a cloud, your sins.

௸ 6 ௸

The Dwelling Place of God

For thus saith the high and lofty One that inhabiteth eternity, whose name is Holy; I dwell in the high and holy place, with him also that is of a contrite and humble spirit. . . .

Isaiah 57:15–16[1]

It is obvious even from a casual reading of this text, that the Lord is speaking about a certain aspect of human life that is extremely important. He is speaking about a heart condition. I could have taken verses out of many parts of the Bible and they would be equally appropriate to describe or to be of assistance in talking about this condition of heart. In Psalm 34 we read that the Lord is ever near unto those who have a broken heart and a contrite spirit (*v. 18*). In Psalm 51 we read that the broken heart is a sacrifice that is pleasing unto the Lord (*v. 17*). It is a sacrifice that He never despises. Psalm 147 tells us that the Lord binds up the wounds of those who are broken in heart (*v. 3*). Then you find a similar statement in my text and again in chapter 66 of Isaiah where it says, 'For all those things hath mine hand made, and all those things have been, saith the Lord: but to this man will I look, even to him that is poor and of a contrite spirit' (v.2). So we find that great emphasis is placed in the Bible on this particular condition of heart.

Perhaps the most marvellous text of all regarding this matter is to be found in Isaiah 61. Christ is here speaking as prophet. These words were true of Himself as he spoke in the synagogue at Nazareth (*Luke 4:16*). The very portion that we read today He read. It is marvellous to think that we can still read the very words that fell from His gracious lips. After the Lord Jesus had read from Isaiah 61 He told the congregation that its words were fulfilled in

[1]January 23, 1977.

Him: 'The Spirit of the Lord God is upon me, because the Lord hath anointed me to preach the gospel to the poor'. And next He said, 'He hath sent me to heal the broken hearted'. Is it not astonishing to think that God the Father sent God the Son from heaven to become incarnate, for this purpose – to bind up those who are broken in heart? He sent Him to make atonement for us by bearing our sins in His own body on the cross. This was not the only reason for which He was sent, for Isaiah goes on to say that He came to 'appoint unto them that mourn in Zion, to give them beauty for ashes, the oil of joy for mourning and the garment of praise for the spirit of heaviness'. I wonder if we know God like that. Is that the kind of God we have and know?

It is a great wonder if any of us escape brokenness of heart, the wounding of the heart, some time or other, in some way or other. This experience comes upon the children of men and nothing can keep it away. But when it comes, what do we do? Where do we go? Have we a God whom we need as a patient needs the doctor or as a sick one needs the nurse who binds up his wounds? Have we one whose personal touch is known to us? Have we one who has pity on our plight and one with whom we are acquainted? I hope that you to whom I now speak have not an unanswering God. I hope that you have not a God who is so remote that you talk to him as if he were in the distance. I hope you have a God who is near, living, warm-hearted, tender, as is the One who says in these very verses, 'I will not contend for ever'. The Psalmist was often broken; the Lord's hand was upon him many a time. His heart was broken, in his family life, and in his kingly life, but he goes on to sing,

> *He will not chide continually*
> *Nor keep His anger still.*

He rejoiced to know that, although God was angry, yet He was not angry all the time, for did He not say, 'I will not contend for ever, neither will I be always wroth'.

Let me throw out these words for a little like a life-line, and give me reason to hope that you will be able to catch it and grasp it. If you feel tonight the pang of the Lord's hand on your heart; if you have gone wrong in your life somewhere; if God has caught up with you and you feel that He is angry with you, well, I would throw out these words to you, 'He will not contend for ever'. Remember these words, and take encouragement from them. Go to the throne of grace and say to God, 'Although Thou dost hide Thy face from me today, Thou wilt not hide it from me tomorrow'. You have every reason to say it. Tomorrow will be better, 'He will not contend for ever'. What a marvellous message this is!

I WHO GOD IS

Here then, coming to the kernel of our text, we have God describing Himself as living in two dwelling places. He is the high and lofty One, dwelling in a holy place, and His own name is Holy. Let us read these truths again, slowly, and meditate on them.

First, He is 'the high and lofty One, who inhabits eternity, whose name is Holy' (spelt with a capital letter). God here tells us that holiness belongs to His very being. Here we get a little insight – a little, because we are so small, so short-sighted – of the immeasureableness and loftiness, the amazing greatness of the almighty God. He is the high and lofty One. He dwells in the lofty places, in heaven above. He describes His own majesty. He describes Himself as dwelling in the sphere of absolute sovereignty, in the sphere of infinite power and omnipotence. Why should we be afraid? Why should you be afraid of the greatest potentate in the whole world, that is, the devil, with all his mysterious power? Why should you be afraid of him? Think instead of One who is higher than he, the lofty One who dwells in the sphere of omnipotence. The devil cannot do anything except that which God allows him to do. So then, we are given this insight into who God is, the Most High!

I remember hearing a preacher say that old people in our West Highlands always addressed God as the Most High in their prayers. He said that there was a great reverence in their approach to God. There is nothing in the world more beautiful than reverence in our approach to God. I confess that if there is anything in this world that makes me shiver, it is to hear the words of an irreverent person. I would rather listen to a heretical sermon than listen to an irreverent prayer. It gives us great pain to listen to a man who brings God down to his own level. We cannot and must not do that. He is the Most High, higher than the angels, higher than the saints; infinitely higher than both angels and men. And then we are to think upon His eternity. That is, of course a dimension beyond our comprehension altogether. God is one who has no beginning and no end. Isaiah says these things as a background for what follows.

II WHERE GOD DWELLS

He says, next, that God dwells somewhere. Of course, God dwells everywhere; He is omnipresent. But the Bible speaks of God having His dwelling place in glory, that is to say, in heaven. Now the strange thing is that God has another place where He dwells, namely, in him who has 'a contrite and humble spirit'. Now I wish I had the power to show you the contrast involved in this – the marvel of it, the condescension of it – that the great and infinite God, whom the heaven of heavens cannot contain, should dwell with the poor in heart, with those whom He calls blessed, 'Blessed are the poor in spirit' (*Matt. 5:3*). What a wonderful God must He be when He can dwell in the contrite, in the poor in spirit, and in the broken hearted!

Now how is this true? Consider, what is it that breaks one's heart? Our hearts naturally are very hard; they are as hard as rock and even harder. But what breaks a heart in the sight of God? To put it very briefly, what breaks the heart of God's child is an understanding of the evil of sin. A person tells a lie, or does not tell the whole truth. What is wrong with that? some people say. I answer, when the eye of the mind is opened by God it sees the evil of every sin in the sight of God. The heart is never broken until it sees sin as God sees it. When a person's heart is truly broken, it never views any sin as small. I do not want to give you the impression that a broken-hearted person is absolutely sinless; that is not the case. He has sin in his heart and sins may be in his life, but he has this characteristic, that he sees sin as it actually is, and he believes what God says about it. He believes in God's discernment of and description of sin.

I heard a horrible thing on the wireless the other night, the most horrible blasphemy. There was nothing wrong with the subject of the talk; it was very interesting; but then, all of a sudden, this horrid blasphemy came out. It was a torrent of blasphemy against God because He let children die, allowed them to be killed on the road, and things like that. Now there are mysteries that we cannot solve. But what we do know is this, that God is just, and the person who is broken in heart knows that God is just. There never was such a thing as an innocent infant. There are innocent children comparatively speaking, but not absolutely speaking. There was only one child who was absolutely innocent, and that was Christ Jesus. He went through life without contracting any sin. He went to the cross as an innocent person and there He bore the wrath of God. The question is not, Is God just because in His providence He allowed a young child to be killed on the road? There are questions far deeper than that! The great question is this: Was God just when He sent His own son to a cursed tree to die for other people, when He Himself had done no wrong? Was God just? The believer with the broken heart knows that God is just. He knows that God is just in all His ways. In the true sense of the word the broken in heart is a humble person. There is no sin more arrogant, more obnoxious to God, than the sin of pride. I mention unbelief often as being the greatest sin, but pride is the inseparable twin sin.

Pride is obnoxious to God, and it is in us all. I do not here refer to people proud of their families or of their jobs. I am talking about people being proud spiritually, proud in the sight of God. This is why there are so many unbelievers in the world. They refuse to bow down to God or to receive submissively the gift of the righteousness of God. God says that if you want to be saved, the only way to be saved is by faith in Jesus Christ. You have to be born again. But unsaved proud people say that they want to be saved in another way, their own way, and the conflict goes on and on. But God never gives way to them; they must submit to His way or perish in their sins. The saved sinner is poor in heart, broken in heart; he is a humble soul in the sight of God. By that I mean, that he comes into the presence of God with nothing whatsoever by way of merit. If you do that, then you are broken in heart. You are a true Christian if you come into the presence of God with nothing to boast of, nothing for which you can claim merit, nothing for which God can grant you favour. Can you do that? Do you know yourself? Do you search yourself to learn you are broken-hearted?

As I go along on the stream of time to eternity, this is one of my greatest comforts, that I know perfectly well when I come into the presence of God or come to Him in prayer, that I come with empty hands.

The Dwelling Place of God

Nothing in my hand I bring,
Simply to Thy cross I cling.

There is much in my heart that I could bring to God by way of
self, but I ask God to suppress me. I pray that He would suppress
me. He does this; and when I come, I come not as a preacher or
minister of a congregation, I come not as a man making a
profession over the years, I come as a man absolutely empty of
anything that is good in and of myself. I count myself empty in the
presence of God; I cast myself into the arms of God and plead the
mercy of God. If you do that, then you can take it that you have a
broken heart. Your heart may have felt at times as hard as a stone,
but God will take out of you the heart of stone and give you a heart
of flesh. He will render you humble. He will fulfil His promises.

But let me go further. What kind of heart do you have tonight in
the presence of your God? Do you remember your sins? Do you
ever shed inward tears for your sins, do you look back on them and
repent of them, in the sight of God? Or have you a heart of stone?
To sorrow to repentance would be a most unnatural thing for you
to do, if you had a heart made of stone. To have a heart of stone is a
most unnatural thing to have but many have such a heart. If
somebody told you that your heart was not a heart of flesh but a
heart of stone what would you think? We read of one in the Old
Testament whose heart became as a stone, and that was the end of
him (*1 Sam 25:37*). Give thought then to this important question.
What is your heart like in the presence of God? If we have a broken
and a contrite heart, God dwells with us in person by His Spirit.
This is a marvellous thing. It shows marvellous condescension on
the part of God. God dwells in our hearts as He dwells in heaven, in
the person of His Spirit.

III WHERE GOD DWELLS WITH APPROBATION

But I must mention something further. Where does God dwell
with approbation? He loves, we read, to dwell with the broken-
hearted. As I have said already, God is everywhere but it is not in
every place that He takes pleasure. God is in the public house – in
every one that is open in Inverness – and He is in the picture
houses. God is there, even as He is in His church, but He is not

there with delight. But we hope He is in this congregation with delight. We hope that it is with complacency that He is with us, but He cannot dwell with delight in evil places. If you went to dwell with somebody you loved most in the world, you would want to stay, you would want to live there. You approve of the person and so you will dwell there. This is what God does. But think for a moment of the two places where God delights to dwell. One place is large, no man can number its inhabitants, God is there, in His glory, in heaven. How large it is we do not know. We know it is a universe, a place of cleanness and sinlessness, and He is there. He is the goodness of it all. In comparison, your heart and my heart are so small, but He dwells in them too. This is by way of comparison: one is perfect and the other is not perfect. There is no sin in heaven. But what can be said of our hearts? Sometimes, I suppose, you put a question mark at this, you doubt if what Scripture says can be true. How can we think that the holy and lofty God will dwell in our heart, in the kind of heart we have. And yet this is what God says. You cannot get beyond it; 'I dwell', He says, 'with him also that is of a contrite and humble spirit'.

But, again, look at the matter further by way of comparison. What goes on in the two places? The same thing goes on in heaven above that goes on in the broken spirit below. What goes on? Let me say, first of all, that I am as sure tonight of what I assert as I am that the Bible is open before me. We do not know much about the activity of those who are glorified in heaven. But we know this, that whatever they are or are not doing, there is an immeasureable adoration of God. Unceasing adoration continues there. On earth too, it is the humble heart and the broken spirit that engages in the adoration of God. We experience interruption, of course, but adoration is there. So then, let me just pick up this thought, for your own sakes: If you adore God on earth then you are doing what the glorified ones do in heaven. You adore God, and you do it because God dwells in your heart. Do you love money more than you love God? Do you love your house more than you love God? Do you boast of other things more than of God? You cannot do so if your heart is a broken heart; you adore God and that is what they do in glory.

Furthermore, I know that in heaven there is constant worship. The glorified fall down before Him who sits on the throne, and they give glory and honour unto Him. They take off their crowns and cast them at His feet. We read all this in the Book of the Revelation. They worship Him who lives for ever and ever. And if God is in your heart, you will worship Him too. It is a characteristic of the broken heart that it worships God. Oh, there are people, and probably there are people listening to me here tonight, and they worship God only on the Sabbath. That is all. They seem to know little of the high and lofty One. And you hear of some people who complain that it is too long for them to worship even for an hour, or an hour and a quarter, far less for a whole day. If God is dwelling in your heart, then you worship God, you want to worship Him. He delights to dwell in you and you delight to worship Him.

But there is another matter to be mentioned: our entire dependence upon God. The mere thought of independence of God is hateful to us. Truly we are utterly dependent upon Him. Abraham was as dependent upon God as you and I are. And being in heaven will not give you independence of God. We are dependent upon God always for everything. It is one of the characteristics of our prayers that we are dependent upon God. Our sufficiency is of God, not of ourselves.

And last (but not least) love must be mentioned. The saints in glory and the angels love God. Of that, there is no doubt. If God dwells in you, you have a broken heart and a contrite spirit, you love God; there is nothing surer than that. If God dwells in your heart you love Him, and He reigns in your heart.

Finally, do you realize that saints on earth and saints in glory are joined together in heart? It is as if there were only a curtain or a wall between them. You hear your neighbour, though he may be unseen; you hear work going on, or speaking, and you know there are people near at hand. If God is in our hearts we are, as it were, in a semi-detached house, and we hear voices from glory. We have evidences that there is another room and one day God will take the wall down and we shall have one complete house. That is what God is going to do for all among us who are broken in heart and contrite in spirit. He will take us to the place where He is, the high and lofty One; you can put it like this, if you like, that your heart will be in heaven and heaven will be in your heart. Either way is comforting. And while we remain here upon earth, what greater comfort can even God Himself give to us than to say, 'With this man I dwell, with him who is of a poor and of a broken spirit'.

But I must say this also, that we are going to part tonight when we go out of this house, and I have to ask this question. Does God dwell in my heart? In the person of the Holy Spirit, does He dwell in your heart? If He does, then you are a true child of God, you are a Christian. And I cannot even begin to mention all that is awaiting you. 'Eye hath not seen, nor ear heard, neither have entered into the heart of man, the things which God hath prepared for them who love him. But God hath revealed them to us by his Spirit.' If God reigns in your heart, nobody knows how much you long for Him. Does He dwell in you? Or is it true, as it was of old, 'Behold, I stand at the door and knock'. What does that mean? It means that He is on the outside, and that there is so much din and noise, so much love to the world and sin, that you are too busy to open the door and let Him in. 'Behold I stand at the door!' With some of you, I believe He has been standing there over many years, knocking. So I will conclude by trying to put terror into you, and in this way; if you leave Him there, outside, if you leave Him standing, knocking, do you know what is going to happen to you? One day you will stand at His door and knock, but He will not let you in! And then it would be better for you if you had never been born. That is what will happen to everyone who keeps Him out; he or she will go to damnation and everyone who welcomes Him in will go to eternal glory.

ᗞᎧ 7 ᗞᎧ

Satisfied

They shall be abundantly satisfied with the fatness of thy house; and thou shalt make them drink of the river of thy pleasures.

Psalm 36:8[1]

The verse has a direct relevance to saved sinners and we find in it a lasting fulfilment of the prophecies and the promises which we have been reading in the prophecy of Isaiah. In chapter 25 we read of the gospel dispensation and what it is like: 'In this mountain shall the Lord of hosts make unto all people a feast of fat things, a feast of wines on the lees, of fat things full of marrow, of wines on the lees well refined'. In these words the superlative joins with the superlative to indicate the riches and fulness of the promises of God in the gospel for those who want to partake. In chapter 55 of the same prophecy we read about 'milk without price, wine without price'. 'Hearken diligently unto me,' says God, 'and eat that which is good, and let your soul delight itself in fatness'. That is the invitation of God to those who are without food. You have no means at all of knowing, experimentally, what goes on in a house unless you go into the house yourself. And the man who wrote the 36th Psalm had gone into the house; he had gone into the place to which God had invited him. He then found out for himself what the Lord's provision for His own people was like, for he tells us in this verse.

David's view of things religious is very different from the popular view. The popular view has been proved to be a lie more often than we can tell, but we cannot convince anybody of that until God Himself shows it to them. The popular view of the Christian life is that it is a morose, dull, dreary, joyless kind of life.

[1]January 25, 1976.

[63]

I would venture to say that there is not anyone in my audience this evening, who at one time did not think of the Christian life in that way. Even if you were brought to the Lord when you were very young, you can remember the times before you were brought to the Lord. You remember in your early days how your parents made you keep the Sabbath Day. They would not let you read any book but a religious one; they would not let you take the toys out to play with them; they would not let you use the Lord's Day as other days, and it seemed to you dreary and long. I remember one of my own sons asking me on one occasion, 'Why did the Lord make the Sabbath Day much longer than the other days?' Well, he was only expressing his feelings in his own way. But this is the way with us all, and then as we grow older we take more part in the pleasures of the world.

I know there is a popular notion that if you are brought up very discreetly; if religion is not forced upon you by your parents; if they are judicious about introducing it, that it will attract the young children of the family and they will come to take to themselves the religion of their parents. 'Do not force religion upon them,' people say. 'Be discreet and wise and psychological in your approach'. We confess that we cannot consider the problem as if ideal parents abounded. We are all children of Adam, we are liable to make mistakes and to do foolish things. David, the man who wrote the Psalm at which we are now looking, had to confess, 'Iniquities prevail against me' (*Psa. 65:3*), and David was a godly man. Many parents have learned to their sorrow how difficult it is, not to bring up their children in their own religion but to bring them *to* their religion. I would remind them that seed, however good, will not grow in a soil if the soil is not congenial. Children may have excellent parents who may bring them up ideally from the Christian point of view. Do you think that is going to put true religion into their childrens' hearts? No, not a bit of it! When religion goes into the heart it is God who puts it there. It is God, and no other, who makes both parents and children know what belongs to true religion.

The popular view of religion is that it has no joy, that it is closely akin to misery. Many people do not want to have it, or to take any part in it; they do not want it to have any effect upon them at all. The devil is ever at work to turn people away from God, and especially young people. He says to them: 'If you become religious and are converted, you will have to forsake lots and lots of things that you now take pleasure in, and what is going to happen to you? You cannot have the friends with whom you associate now. You will have to give up your dancing, to leave your present style of life, and to abandon all sorts of pleasures, revellings, and drunkenness maybe. Surely you are not going to spend the rest of your life like that!' The devil is a deceiver, the father of lies, and that is how he puts things.

But the view of those who find true religion is very different from that of the devil. The Psalmist assures us that the Lord's people will be abundantly satisfied with the fatness of His house and will be made to drink of the river of His pleasures. That is a great thing to say. Let us then, spend a little time in thinking of these things.

'They shall be filled with the fatness of thy house': it is a wonderful phrase, a pleasant phrase – 'the fatness of thy house'. It was borrowed from the tabernacle days when people used to bring their offerings to the altar and there were certain regulations concerning 'the fat of their offering'. We all know that the fat is the richest part of the meat. That is why certain regulations were made under the Old Testament economy, and also why riches – riches of grace – are often referred to as 'fatness'. 'They shall be filled with the fatness of thy house.'

I THE HOUSE OF GOD

First of all, what is the house of God in which this fatness is to be found? I am going to speak of it from four different points of view.

1. *The Church itself*

First of all, the house of God is not a place like the building we are now in, made of stone and mortar. I agree, this building is specially erected for worship on Sabbath and on weekdays, and we often call it 'the house of God'. And rightly so! But the real house of God is the church itself – the living organism, the body of believers in whom the Lord dwells and works, the hearts in which the Holy Spirit operates, bringing them to feed abundantly on the bread which He provides from the fulness of His house. No living member of this body is excluded. And that is what is chiefly meant in the Bible by 'the house of God'.

There are several reasons for what I have just asserted. One of them is that there is the presence of God always. When and where there is a Christian then and there is the presence of God; and where there is a gathering of Christians there, and there particularly, is the presence of God. 'Where two or three are gathered together in my name, there am I in the midst of them' (*Matt. 18:20*). That is what God says, and if you and I value the presence of the Lord we shall find it where two or three are gathered together in His name. The operative phrase is 'gathered in my name'. It is not, where two or three Christians are gathered together, or even where two or three thousand Christians are gathered together, all of them true Christians, without a gathering of them in the name of the Lord. But the word says, 'Where two or three are gathered together *in my name*, there am I in the midst of them'. And if we want to see and to feel the presence of the Lord, that is where we can experience it – where two or three are gathered together in His name. Then, too, there is the operation of the Spirit of God. Where there are Christian people, the Spirit of God operates in their hearts. These are the things which characterize the church of God and the living members of the church of God.

2. The Word of God

We must further think of the 'fatness of God's house' as it is found in the Word of God, in every aspect of it. Think of this Word as containing God's promises, as containing His precepts and as concerning the eternal principles of true religion. The Word is full of fatness in all these aspects. Think, I say, of the 'exceeding great and precious promises' of God found in His Word. Have you ever got a promise from God? If so, you will value it more than if you had got all the world's riches; you will be richer than Andrew Carnegie ever was. One promise from the Word of God! Paul thought that when he listed the things that were against him at the time of his trouble. God gave him a promise, 'My grace is sufficient for thee' (*2 Cor. 12:9*). And, you know, if God gives you a promise, it uplifts your whole life; you walk as it were on air once the Lord gives you a promise. It makes you as 'bold as a lion' (*Prov. 28:1*). The world does not worry you; it can do you no harm. The promise of God is a pleasant thing to the believing soul. It is full of happiness.

Then there are the precepts of the Lord in His Word, and they too are extremely precious. You find this stated in Psalm 119 and in many other parts of the Bible. The principles, too, contained in the Word of God, are well worth studying, everyone of them, and they are full of fatness. People often ask: 'Do you think a Christian should do this or do that? Is it right for a Christian to smoke? Should a Christian go to a concert of classical music?' And there are many other such questions. The Bible does not mention these things by name, of course, but I am persuaded that if you read the Bible properly and prayerfully you will never have a problem in your mind which is not answered either by the explicit directions and directives, or by the principles of the Word of God. I am convinced that there is an answer in the Bible for every perplexity and problem that arises, and if the Bible does not say anything by way of precept concerning smoking as it does about stealing – 'Thou shalt not steal' – the answer to the question as to whether a Christian ought to smoke or not, will be found in the principles of the Bible. Search out those principles for yourselves in the Bible. They concern every aspect of our lives. And do not look upon problems in a merely general way but as they concern yourself. Do not say, 'Is it right for Christians to smoke?' but say, Is it right for me to smoke? Should I attend this or that place? Should I do this or refrain from that? Apply the principles to yourself, and read the Bible not to find out what it says to other people, but what it says to *you* first and foremost.

3. Gospel Ordinances

But I must speak a word about gospel ordinances and upon the public means of grace. God 'loves the gates of Zion more than all the dwellings of Jacob' (*Psa. 87:2*). 'They that feared the Lord spake often one to another . . . and a book of remembrance was written before him for them that feared the Lord, and that thought upon his name' (*Mal. 3:16*). There is something in the ordinances of the gospel and in the open public means of grace that you do not get in other places. The presence of the Lord and the fatness of His house are not confined to the public means of grace, but I repeat, that there is something in the public means of grace, concerning the fatness of God's house that you will not get anywhere else. Try it for yourself; put it to the test. Can I get as much pleasure from staying at home and listening to a sermon on the wireless instead of going to church? Try it and see. You belong to the Free Church. Supposing there is a Free Church minister preaching on the wireless in the morning or evening, and you stay at home and listen to the service. Do you get as much pleasure from it, as much profit, as you would in coming to the public means of grace, that is, if you are able to come to them? Try it and see! Can anything at all be put in the place of what God has appointed for the feeding of your soul? The plain answer is, No! The public means of grace are the appointment of God and these are full of fatness for the believing soul.

4. Divine Provision

Another thing I would mention regarding the house of God is that the house of God is a divine provision for every soul in need. There was once a young man who had to flee from his father's house, out of fear of his life. When evening arrived he could not go further on his journey that day, so he lay down to sleep at the spot where he found himself. There he dreamed and he never forgot it. And this is what he said about it, 'This is none other but the house of God, and the gate of heaven' (*Gen. 28:17*). If Jacob found his Bethel in the wild, waste desert to be the house of God you will find Him in desert places too. Moses was in the wilderness and one day he was occupied with his shepherding of the flock. That was all he was doing, taking care of the flock for his father-in-law. Then something he saw startled him – a burning bush! He said, 'I will now turn aside and see this great sight, why the bush is not burnt' (*Exod. 3:3*). And there, he and the Lord held converse together, a conversation that altered the history of the whole world. Something must be accomplished that had to do with the whole work of redemption. And there, in the wilderness, Moses found the house of God. Elijah, in despondency, fled from Jezebel and went for forty days into a wilderness. While he was there, there came an earthquake and a wind and then the still small voice of God spoke to him. The Lord, it is said, was not in the earthquake, but what that means is not that it was not the Lord who caused it, but that he did not speak to Elijah during the time of the earthquake (*1 Kings*

19:11). Indeed, the Lord is in all these things, He gave to Elijah of the fatness of His house. He had just given him bread to eat that nobody had ever baked.

Come to the New Testament and think of Paul and Silas in the prison with their feet held fast in the stocks. And in the middle of the night – and it was not for a show – their hearts were so full of joy that they began singing praises to God. The prison cell was probably miry and dirty; there were criminals around; their bodies were bruised with the beating that they had received that day; and yet they sang praises to God. To them the prison was the house of God (*Acts 16:25*). They were far happier than was Caesar in his palace. Or take another example. There is an island called Patmos, not far from Ephesus to which the Apostle John was sent just to keep his mouth shut – to keep him from preaching the gospel. If any man ever had the 'house of God' in his banishment, John the Apostle had it. On lonely Patmos! And to Christians today any place can become 'the house of God'. Your bedroom, your living room, outside on the mountains, following your employment, out in your fishing boat – it does not matter where – when the Lord gives you His presence in a special way, you are filled with the 'fatness of his house'. In ordinary common experiences, in bereavement, in sickness, sorrow, loneliness, in things that we are afraid of – even as we go through these experiences we find them to be 'the house of God'. Such is the presence of God that we would not have missed the experience on any account because of His presence. We have been filled with the fatness of His house.

II THE FATNESS OF THE HOUSE

A word next about the fatness of the house. What is this fatness? There are various ways in which we can think of it.

1. First of all, there is the life of the house

That is mentioned in the verse following our text: 'For with thee is the fountain of life'. In order to experience the fatness of the house you must both enter into the house and you must live in it, and it is because you live that you enter into the house by the light that you get from God. We shall not dwell on that aspect just now, but we certainly know that with God alone is the fountain of life. It is God who gives us life and the things in life that are truly good. They all flow from the fountain of life. God also gives you the desire for the fare of His house, for these provisions which He has provided for our feeding and our nourishment.

2. Another aspect of the quality of the house is the love that is enjoyed there

Love is the fruit of the Spirit; it is not the first fruit of the Spirit, but it certainly is the most delightful of all. It is definitely the sweetest fruit of all. To love is sweeter than to believe. It is not more important, it does not come before faith, but to love is sweeter to the experience than to believe. You can believe without being emotionally stirred, but when you do believe then your emotions are affected and you begin to love. There is nothing sweeter than to love, except one thing, and that is to be loved by a brother or sister, and above and before all, by the Lord Himself. And that is exactly the fatness of the Lord's house. This is the beauty of it and the sweetness of it – that we loved Him because He first loved us. You get an assurance of the love of God to your soul and there is no love in the world sweeter than that. You get a feeling that you are loved by God; it is a heavenly kind of feeling. Such assurance is the fatness of His house. And is not such an experience and such a knowledge better to you than all the gold and silver in the world? Would not you rather know tonight that God loves you, be assured of it, and feel that you love Him more than you love anybody else in the world and more than you could possibly love anybody else? This is love that far excels all other love. It is the fatness of His house.

3. Another thing is the security of God's house

Nothing enters into the house of God which is not pure, at least not with God's approval. True Christians are always cleansed. There was a laver at the door of the tabernacle, full of water, and the priests, when they went in, always washed in the laver. This was an essential. So, too, there is a cleansing needed for the house of the Lord, and this is a part of its blessedness, part of the fatness of His house – that you are cleansed, washed and robed, just as in the parable of the prodigal son. The cleansing is part of the fatness of God's house. Think of what sin means to your conscience when you are not fully conscious of its removal. Even if nobody else knows about it, your conscience accuses you, roaring like a lion. It tells you of your sin; it shows you the awfulness of your sin and the filthiness of your sin. You are lashed by it and oppressed by it. You think that everybody knows it and that everybody is looking at you, and you say, 'my sin is greater than I can bear'. But then, all of a sudden, the Lord washes you in His house and makes you clean. Is that not fatness?

4. There is the fatness of nourishment

Think of the bread that you get in His house. What does that indicate? What you actually get is Christ, nothing less than Christ. Jesus says, 'I am the bread of life' (*John 6:35*). He says, 'If any man thirst, let him come unto me and drink' (*John 7:37*). And in giving us drink from His own cup he gives us Himself. Jesus Christ Himself is the fountain of life. At His bidding we stoop down and drink and live.

Do you know what it is to live on Jesus? It is far easier, really, than that term sounds. It is a term that baffled the learned Jews. They said 'How can this man give us His flesh to eat?' Only the believer in Jesus knows the answer to their question. You get His flesh to eat when, by faith in Him, you know that His death on the cross has become your salvation. That is how you are fed. Jesus died on the tree, and you know that He died for you and secured you life thereby. That is what feeds you. You are able to say, the incarnate Son of God, God of very God, man of very man, died for *me*. When you contemplate these things, the spirit that God put into you, the immortal soul, begins to get fed, and fed with the contemplation of who Christ is, and of what Christ did.

III THE ABUNDANCE

And then there is abundance in Christ and untold riches in Him: 'the fatness of His house' and 'rivers of pleasure'. In this world the rivers have a terrible habit of running dry. Yes, even the sweetest rivers have a habit of turning dry. They are like the brook Cherith to Elijah. He ran to the brook and then the brook dried up. Many a man and woman going through life have had this to say of the sweetest brook in their lives, that the brook ran dry. But these rivers of God's house never dry up – never. They are rivers coming from the throne of God and of the Lamb, and should you not get something in one of them, you will get something in another. If you do not get something in my sermon, you will get something in the rivers of the Word. You will get it in the rivers of secret prayer. There are various rivers of pleasures, and you will get something out of one of them; they will never go completely dry. Then too there is the abundance we receive while sitting at the table of the King where there is always enough to spare and where we 'shew the Lord's death till he come'.

And notice that this abundance is altogether heavenly in its nature. The pleasures are *God*'s pleasures. The Psalmist tells us so, he writes of 'the river of thy pleasures'. When you are enjoying the fatness of the house of God, God is giving you as your joy the very thing that gives Him joy. If I come into the house of God and partake of this fatness, I get my joy out of the very thing from which God gets joy. It is almost too much to be believed. Perhaps some of you think I am carrying things too far, and that I am overbold in my statement, but I am not. This is exactly what happens. Is it not written in the Bible that the Lord takes pleasure in His people? If you had to spend an evening, say watching television, watching something cultural or educational, or if you had to stay with somebody who could speak well about the things of earth but who did not know Christ and would not talk to you about Christ, would you prefer any one of these things to conversation with a converted person who would talk of Christian experience? I ask again, which would you prefer, which would you find more sweet in your soul? I have no doubt that if you and I delight in the fatness of God's house, we would find our true pleasure in the people of the Lord.

And there is another thing to which the Psalmist refers, another thing in which the Christian gets joy of God. Supposing you heard of a sinner who is converted – and you do hear that sometimes, if you have ears, although far too seldom in our day – what effect has it upon you? Is it just like an ordinary bit of news? Let me tell you something that Jesus said, concerning the lost sheep brought back to the fold, and the lost coin sought for and found: 'Likewise there is joy in the presence of the angels of God over one sinner that repenteth' (*Luke 15:10*). If I am filled with the fatness of the Lord's house, it means that I have the same joy, the same kind of joy in the conversion of a sinner that there is in heaven in the presence of the angels of God – 'Thou shalt make them drink of the river of thy pleasures'.

It is a marvellous thing to know that there is such a concord between God and man. Enoch walked with God and so do you walk with God. When He gives you of His own pleasures, and you take pleasure in what He takes pleasure in, you are at one with God. And then there is satisfaction! I began by saying that His house is full of joy. It does not matter what the world gives you, it does not matter how much you take out of the world; your stay on earth may be one long life of pleasure without any ingredient of pain or sorrow or bereavement. Though no life is really like that. But supposing it was like that, what of the end? What about the day of reckoning? What do you expect in that day? The joy of the Christian lies in this – he enjoys the fatness of God's house. It does not matter what else he is deprived of, it does not matter what his losses are, in the end all will be well with him. He is secure. When God's angels of judgment come forth to separate the righteous from the wicked, they will see the blood of redemption sprinkled upon his conscience and upon his heart; he will not be banished by the justice or judgment of God. The resolve of such a man, nailed as it were over his door, is this: 'in God is all that I want in this world, and He is far more to me than wealth, wife and children, and everything else that can be put together, a thousand times over'. If God sees this above the door of my life and heart then I can say, 'there is now no condemnation', destruction will never come in. It does not matter how poor the house is providentially; it does not matter how small it is; it does not matter how bare the cupboard and the shelves. With that written on the door for God to see, and for me to know, I will rejoice and will dance for joy and will continue to do so with all my might. It is all I want if God is for me. That is the main element of the fatness of the house. There is so much here in this Psalm for you to think over. Will you not enter then into the house of the Lord? Enter by the door, by Jesus Christ, and you will know it all for yourself.

∾ 8 ∾

The Presence of God

Cast me not away from thy presence.

Psalm 51:11[1]

The history of this Psalm is so well-known that I need not spend any time talking about it. Volumes have been written upon it, people will be talking about it as long as there is a world, and yet the matter of it can never be exhausted. It records a sacred experience and we can only touch the fringe of it as it were. There are many who can understand it, especially those who have gone through the same kind of experiences by way of penitence. They know to a large extent what the Psalmist is saying, and they understand the manner in which he is saying it. If ever language was the expression of a broken heart and a contrite spirit, it is the language which believers can take up from this Psalm, for many of them are not strangers to such an experience as this. When they repent of their sins they make in effect the same kind of prayer that David prayed.

First of all I must call attention to what the prayer does not mean, and then to what it does mean.

What the prayer does not mean is this: The Psalmist does not pray that he may be cast away from what we describe in theological language as the essential presence of God. The Psalmist knew that God was omnipresent. God would not be God if He were not everywhere at one and the same time. Omnipresence is one of His properties. The Psalmist knew that very well. Does he not express it in Psalm 139:

> *From thy spirit whither shall I go*
> *Or from thy presence flee?*

[1]January 26, 1975.

The omnipresence of God implies His infinite knowledge of all things, of all deeds, of all thoughts, of all words. The Psalmist does not say, 'Cast me not out of that presence', for that were an impossibility. God cannot do that and remain God. If there were anything that He did not see or did not know, then He would not be the infinite God. We all know this, if we believe in God at all. So the Psalmist in his prayer does not mean that God should cast him somewhere where He is not. It cannot mean that. In that sense God cannot cast anyone from His presence. Furthermore, God's presence in the sense of omnipresence, in the sense of Him being God and knowing all things, is not in one place more than in another. He is not more present in heaven than He is in hell. Be very careful at this point not to misunderstand me. I remember a happening many years ago, before I moved to Inverness. Some-body came to me when I was in Urray. He had been at a Communion season in another place and said that he heard the minister say that God's presence was in hell. Either the minister did not explain what he meant, or else this person was not intelligent enough to grasp what the minister was saying. The matter is quite clear to a Christian who thinks biblically. God's presence cannot be in one place more than in another. God is as much in the worst place that you can think of in the world, as He is in this congregation that has assembled to worship. He is not any more present in the gathering of angels and saints in glory than He is in hell among the lost, in as far as His essential presence is concerned. We have to qualify the statement in this way. God's presence in hell does not make hell into a heaven; His presence in the worst place does not make it a sacred place; but His presence is there nevertheless. So far, we take note of what the prayer does not mean. We now came to talk about what it does mean.

What the Psalmist means in Psalm 51 by the presence of God, is the favour or the grace or the delight that God takes in a soul. 'Cast me not away from thy presence' – from Thy grace, from Thy complacency, from taking delight in me. Cast me not away from Thee in that way. That is what the Psalmist means. And if we take hold of this, then we can understand in a measure what the prayer implies. The favour of God is not everywhere. It is not in hell. It is not in the company of the wicked where God's presence is in the sense of His favour and grace. Where God's presence is not in the other world, there is hell. As we have already seen, God is there

[75]

essentially, but He is not there with His favour, with His grace, and that is what makes hell a hell. And this is what the Psalmist means.

1. First of all I would say that this is the prayer of a good man, of a godly man

Now let us for a moment pause while I put a question to everyone of us: Did you ever pray with all your heart that God would not cast you away from His favour? If you have done so, then you are a godly person. You are converted. You are a child of God. And you need no other evidence than that; it is sufficient. But I put the question to you again: Did you ever ask this, 'Cast me not away from Thy grace, from Thy favour?' Did you ever ask the Lord, 'Whatever comes upon me in this life, let this not come on me, that I shall be cast away from Thy favour, from Thy grace'? If you asked that, then you asked a good thing. And your asking it shows you are a godly person. The difference between the godly and the ungodly is shown in this way. What the ungodly want most of all is to be cast away from the presence of God. That is what Adam wanted when he sinned; he went and hid himself among the trees of the garden. Cain's punishment was that he was cast out from the presence of the Lord. The wicked in this world want this more than anything; they hope that God does not see them and that they can get away from Him, where He is not, if there were such a place. But you do not want that if you are a child of God. You say 'Cast me not away from thy presence'. But some quick-minded person may say to me, 'Is it not said concerning Jonah, and he was a good man, that he "fled from the presence of the Lord"?' That is so but it is meant in a different sense. Jonah was fleeing away from his duty. God told him to do something he did not want to do and he ran away from the duty that was put upon him. He was not fleeing from the presence of the Lord because he hated the presence of the Lord. That is what the wicked do, but a godly man will never do so. He will never hate the presence of the Lord.

Why did I say that the Psalmist's prayer was the prayer of a godly man? Because I have scriptural warrant for it, in many parts of the Bible. I will mention some of them. Think of the Psalms. 'One thing have I desired of the Lord, that will I seek after; that I may dwell in the house of the Lord all the days of my life, to behold the beauty of the Lord, and to enquire in his temple' (*Psa. 27:4*). 'I had rather be a doorkeeper in the house of my God, than to dwell in the tents of wickedness' (*Psa. 84:10*). We find the same thing in Psalm 42 where the Psalmist longs for the house of the Lord and mourns that he cannot get to that house. Again, the theme is found in the prophecy of Jeremiah. 'Why', says the prophet, 'shouldest thou be as a stranger in the land, and as a wayfaring man that turneth aside to tarry for a night?' (*Jer. 14:8*). The prophet longed for God's presence. 'Oh that I knew where I might find him!' says Job, 'that I might come even to his seat!' (*Job 23:3*) 'Oh that thou wouldest rend the heavens, that thou wouldest come down', says Isaiah (*Isa. 84:1*) I could go on and on, showing you how the godly long for the presence of their God.

2. *The second thing I notice is that this is the prayer of a penitent man*

Godly men are penitent men. And here is a man who is penitent, who mourns for his sin. He has a consciousness of having grieved God and the Holy Spirit. So he says, 'Cast me not away from thy presence'. His consciousness of sin made him afraid that God would deal with it and bring upon him the greatest judgment of all, that of being cast away from His presence. The man who prayed this prayer did not doubt his interest in Christ, for he had been assured from the mouth of the prophet Nathan that his sin had been forgiven. And yet he says, 'Cast me not away from thy presence'. So if you say, 'Cast me not away from thy presence', do not think that it is an evidence that you are not a Christian. And do not think that it is inconsistent to pray in this way and at the same time to hold on to your interest in Christ. You have the example of the Psalmist to support you. No, although the Psalmist had a consciousness of sin, he abhors the thought of being cast away from the presence of the Lord.

Directly or indirectly, sin is the only thing that can rob a person of the Lord's presence. We see it in the case of Adam and Eve. They lived in the presence of the Lord, having His grace and favour, but they sinned and God cast them out from His presence. They were cast out of the garden, cast out of His presence; they forfeited God's favour by reason of their sin. Or take the case of Samson who was a good man. But he sinned and one day he found that he was cast out of the presence of the Lord. Sin had caused it.

The Bible contains many such examples. They cause godly men to cry, 'Cast me not away from Thyself'. Nothing but sin can cause this casting away, directly or indirectly, some way or other, and it was sin that made the Psalmist utter the prayer.

Sometimes God gives the feeling that one is cast away from His presence in order to try a person's faith. We have examples of this in Scripture. Job was never cast out of the presence of the Lord although he thought he was; but his faith was being tried. And it was not because of any fault in Job's life that this happened to him. It was a trial of his faith and he was not directly responsible for it. Think of the case of the Syrophoenician woman who came to ask mercy of God for her daughter, but at first Christ answered her never a word. How did she respond? Did she say, 'I cried to Him with all my heart and He never allowed me to think that He had heard me. I am cast out of His presence'? If she said that in her heart, she was entirely wrong. Oh how He pitied her although she did not know it! But then, when He spoke at all, He said: 'I am not sent but to the lost sheep of the house of Israel . . . It is not fit to take the children's bread and to cast it to dogs' (*Matt. 15:24–26*). Must she then say, 'I am cast out of His presence'? If she thought that, nobody was ever more wrong in a conclusion. The fact was, that nobody was ever so near to His heart as she was at that very moment. But that is *not* what she thought. And you might feel that you are cast out of His presence when it is not so.

But there is another thing we must notice. When the Psalmist says, 'Cast me not out of thy presence', he does not find any fault with God should He cast him away. The first thing that an ungodly man does when God does not deal with him as he wants Him to do, is to find fault with Him. He says, 'Why does God do it, why? Why does God do that?' And such thoughts are in us all. But these thoughts come, I hope, not to lodge in our hearts; they come and we cannot keep them out, but we do not give them lodging. God forbid! No, the godly man says, 'Cast me not away from thy presence', recognizing that if God were to do it, He would be doing just the right thing. He says: 'I have sinned against God, and if God were to do this to me, He would only be acting in strict accord with His own law. I have sinned and my sin deserves this terrible judgment. And if God brings judgment upon me, God is acting righteously.' Now, friend, did you ever say that? Let me say this for your comfort. If you say to yourself – 'Here I am, and I am in a bad way; I am in a dreadful mess, I have sinned against God and I reap misery and sorrow and anguish. I reap misery night and day. My tears have been my meat both night and day. But God is right, I deserve it. I deserve it for my sin' – if you say that, if you do not find fault with God because of all the miseries you are in but trace these to your sins, then I say you do this because you are a godly man. Nobody acts in this way but a godly person. Believe me then and take comfort from the words of the Psalmist.

3. Then again, the prayer before us is the prayer of one who believes in the terms of the everlasting covenant

This is quite obvious. One of the doctrines of the Bible is that of the final perseverance of the saints. The Psalmist knew very well, and I hope we know it too, that once a person comes into the favour of God, once he gets the grace of God in his heart, he will never go out of the favour of God. God's grace will never be taken out of his heart. That person is as safe from the day he is converted as Abraham is in the sight of the throne of God. If you are a Christian today you are as safe as if you were in heaven. You will one day be in heaven; there is no doubt about that. We speak of this as one of the points of Calvinism; it is certainly one of the things the Scripture teaches; it is impossible for you to fall from grace. David knew that well. Is not that what he said as his death drew near? He said, 'My house is not right with God; everything has gone against me, yet He hath made with me an everlasting covenant, that it would never be broken'.

I mention this in answer to the words we have just been singing in the service.

> *Forever will the Lord cast off,*
> *And gracious be no more.*
> *Forever is His mercy gone*
> *Fails His word evermore?*

The Psalmist, reflecting on what he was thinking, said, 'This is my infirmity' – 'It is because I am so infirm, because I am so full of weakness, that I am like that. I should never have asked these questions. Is it true that the Lord has forgotten to be gracious? I should never have said that, I said it because of my infirmity'. And then he got out of that ditch and said, 'but I will remember the years of the right hand of the most High' (*Psa. 77:10*). He feared God and it is the person who fears God who says, 'Cast me not away from thy presence'. Of course, he feared the coming Judgment. But again, notice that the Psalmist does not say, 'Do not take away thy presence from me'. David does not say that because the presence of God had been taken away from him. What he says is, 'Cast me not away from thy presence', and that is an entirely different thing from the presence of God being taken away. The two things are entirely different. The presence of God can be taken away from you and will be taken away from you if you sin against God. 'If we say that we have fellowship with him, and walk in darkness, we lie, and do not the truth' (*I John 1:6*).

But what the Psalmist says is, '*Cast* me not away'. What kind of things are usually cast away? When you women cast anything away probably it is when you do the spring cleaning. I suppose you throw many things away because you have no more use for them. They have served their usefulness and they are thrown away. What you throw away from you is something that you do not value anymore. This is what the Psalmist meant when he cried, 'Cast me not away from thy presence.' 'Do not look upon me as being utterly useless and of no value any more. Do not throw me away from Thy presence.'

We must remember that at the time the Psalmist used such words he did not possess the conscious presence of God. He was not enjoying God's favour in his soul; he was not enjoying communion with God; he was not sitting in the Lord's banqueting house. He had not the enjoyment of such a favour as that, but he wanted God not to despise him, not to forsake him for ever. For that he was praying.

If God were to cast us away from His presence, what would that mean for us? First of all, it would mean that we would not have divine strength to support us in affliction. I have often said to the one who is truly a Christian, do not worry about what may come into your life; do not worry about it one little bit, and I want to impress this upon you again. You may lose everything that you have in the world; you may have circumstances in your life which are difficult to bear; you may lose your health; many troubles may come upon you; do not worry about that if you are true Christians – none perish that trust in the Lord. But possibly you will worry that you will not have the presence of God in your circumstances. I can assure you of this: that if you have the presence of God in your circumstances, then the circumstances do not matter. Job lost everything; he lost even the goodwill of his wife; he lost the comfort of his friends; they only embittered his sorrow. But he said 'I know that my Redeemer liveth'. 'I *know* it' (*Job 19:25*). 'He knows the way that I take' (*Job 23:10*). Job never lost his grip of the fact that God was with him.

My friends, do you not desire that this should also be the case with you? Who is better off – the man who has not a penny to his name, but who has the presence of God or the man who is as rich as Rockefeller but is without God's presence? Who is better off – the man who is dying of cancer but enjoying the presence of God, or the man who is in perfect health but is living in ungodliness? I say again, who is the better off? Which would you rather be? If the choice lay with you, would you rather be today in hospital dying of a malignant growth and knowing that there is no hope for you but with the presence of God in your soul, or would you prefer to be a man in good health with everything going well with him but destitute of the presence of God? There is no comparison between the two, none at all! If you have the presence of God, you will have the strength for your affliction whatever it be. So no wonder this man says 'Cast me not away from thy presence.' The godly man enjoys such a multitude of blessings that I have not the time to mention them all.

If you are godly, you will be safe when temptations come. You will have power in the conflict with sin, if you have the presence of the Lord. How weak you are if you have not His presence and how strong you are with it! Think again of Samson, the man whom I have mentioned already. He was bound with green withs and with ropes and he broke them as if they were burnt with fire. Why? Because he still retained his hair and God was with him. But later when they bound him with ropes and his hair had been cut, and God had departed from him, he was as helpless as any other man. We too will have power in the conflict with evil, we too will have fervour in our devotion, if God's presence is with us, 'Cast me not from thy presence'.

My friend, what is the case with you? If you give attention to devotions, if you pray and read the Bible, and God is not in your prayer or in the reading of the Bible, then there is something wrong, and for God's sake go and think on it and put it right. If you are cast away from the presence of God, ask that He would restore you to His favour and give you communion with Him. If you are a professed Christian do not call yourself that any more until you get into the favour of God, because this is the sign of real Christianity. God's favour and grace are a guarantee of eternal safety. They produce joy in the Christian life, joy even in tribulation. And with joy you receive clear evidence of His love to you and evidence of His life in your soul.

Two more thoughts and with them I will end. If today you say, 'I feel as if God has cast me out of His presence', what are you going to do? Let me tell you what to do, for you are still within reach of mercy. Come into the presence of the Lord and He will receive you. Even if He has cast you away from Himself, He can and will bring you back again. 'Ah', you say, 'that is strong language, why do you say that?' Because I remember the scene at Calvary where this actually happened to the divine Substitute, mine and yours, the Lord Jesus Christ. As he hung on that cross He cried out, 'My God, why hast thou forsaken me?' God had cast Him out of His presence. And because He did that for Jesus as the Substitute for sinners, if you come through the Substitute He will receive you.

And my last word is this. What need you have of watchfulness and prayer! 'Cast me not away'. Here is a man who used to enjoy the favour of God, but he ceased to be watchful and to be prayerful; down he went, and in Psalm 51 we see how he reaped misery and despair. O friend, watch and pray lest you enter into temptation! Watch and pray!

ୠ **9** ୠ

Affliction

*For our light affliction, which is but for a moment, worketh for us a far
more exceeding and eternal weight of glory: While we look not at the things
which are seen, but at the things which are not seen; for the things which are
seen are temporal; but the things which are not seen are eternal.*

2 Corinthians 4:17–18[1]

This is a marvellous passage of Scripture for it brings us face to
face with the difference between true Christianity and everything
else in the world. I hope you have already discovered what religion really means, and what religion really does. People who have
religion have that which does something for them. If you have a
religion, or seem to have one, that does nothing for you, that does
not change you, that is no different from that which belongs to
the world, the sooner you get away from it the better. Get true
religion in its place. Get the one religion that is true.

Long ago, we are told, chemists and others spent very much
time trying to turn base metal into gold. They thought that in
some way or other they would discover how other metals could be
turned into gold, but they never succeeded. Now this is exactly
what I am going to talk about tonight. The fact that the Christian
religion, the religion of Christ in one's heart and mind, turns that
which is base into that which is priceless, ought to govern everything in your life. True Christianity makes bitter things most
sweet; it turns the most cruel into the most meek; it makes you a
different person and enables you to face the difficulties in life
which we all encounter. The Christian religion in one's heart is
like that latent friend that Samson had when a lion came against
him. With nothing in his hands he rent him asunder. And if we
have the

[1]October 17, 1976.

[83]

grace of God in our hearts and a lion comes with us, we have that latent in our heart which is able to grapple with the lion and slay it.

This is what Paul means in my text. And indeed he is not talking as a man who does not know. When you hear a person talking, you soon discover whether he knows what he is talking about, and whether his words carry any weight. If a man is talking about something he has not experienced, his words will not carry much weight. I knew a man in my native place who had a tremendous gift of memory and a rare gift of language. He could speak of the ships that go to all parts of the world. He could describe the work done aboard these ships, from the Captain downwards, with all the tasks that had to be undertaken and how they were done. He would also describe the ports where the ships landed. And all this he never saw, but from the Minch! Those who knew him knew that he was only passing on information that he had derived from others. His talk carried no weight, but he could tell the facts far better than some who had the experience of what he described.

Paul the Apostle was a total contrast with 'the man of the Minch'. He was a man of great experience from the time of his conversion when the Lord had said to him, 'I will show you what great things you must suffer for my name's sake.' That is the language of Christianity. Would you have been a Christian tonight if the Lord had earlier shown you that to become a Christian you would have to suffer great things for Him? Would that not put you off? It did not put Paul off when great troubles began to assault him one by one. They only served, as the storms served the cedars of Lebanon, to root him deeper and deeper in the Lord Jesus Christ. He never complained and he certainly never gave up. Here in my text the Apostle makes one of the profoundest statements that ever came from his pen. Nobody thought of saying anything like this before; nobody could ever say it but a Christian. Mohammed never said anything like this, nor did Buddha nor any other of those men who have founded false religions. They never said that the trials of life were going to work for their followers a far more exceeding and eternal weight of glory. Confucius, and others like him, were worldly-wise people, who told their fellows to face trials stolidly and with nobility of spirit, but they never said anything like this. It never occurred to them that those things which are the hardest and bitterest will always work for the good of our souls. Nor did they know anything of the Christian faith and of the divine assurance that, for true believers, afflictions are working a far more exceeding and eternal weight of glory.

I THE BELIEVER'S VIEW OF AFFLICTION

We shall consider first of all the believer's view of affliction:

1. Paul regards afflictions as appointed by divine providence

We cannot get this truth properly into our heads except by the grace of God. Such troubles as we meet with so often come upon us unexpectedly. That is not an accident of Providence. Our trials have been fore-ordained by an all-wise God, just as surely as was Christ's coming into the world and His death upon the Cross. That is the believer's view of affliction. Looking at afflictions from this perspective, would you wish that the birth of Christ, the sufferings of Christ, and the death of Christ should never have happened? You shrink back from such a thought, for you now know something about them and their tremendous significance. I say, then, that you ought to have the same view of your afflictions, as you have of the sufferings and death of Christ. As Christ's sufferings and death were fore-ordained by His Father, so have your own trials and afflictions – for the Apostle describes them as afflictions – appointed by God for your eternal good. I want to take you right to the heart of this matter. Do not allow yourself to be tempted to look upon your trials as an accident or as happenings that are not in the providence of God, apart from God Himself. Providence is never apart from God Himself. Not a sparrow falls to the ground without His knowledge. Everything that causes you pain and hurt in your soul or your body, in your family or in your community, is all fore-ordained. Do not complain and do not give up.

2. Paul tells us here that adversity has its effects upon us, that is, if it is long and hard

I am not talking about superficial trials but of the deeper trials of life, trials of which the writer in Proverbs says, 'a wounded spirit who can bear?' Some people go through life and, if I may use the expression, their spirits are as if they were cut with a sword. They live with a broken heart. When such troubles are hard and prolonged, they affect the body and the entire person. The body and the mind alike feel the stress. Paul says about it: 'For which cause we faint not; but though our outward man perish, yet the inward man is renewed day by day.' By the outward man, he means the body that perishes by reason of the load of affliction which it has to bear, and which causes it to decay more quickly than is normal. People who bear these heavy loads sometimes come to a premature grave, although that is not always the case. In my text, Paul sees the Christian man as bearing a load of affliction and enduring suffering thereby in the 'outward man'.

3. Paul also tells us that afflictions renew the inward man

They actually revive him. We cannot understand this unless it is revealed to us. That which tends to kill the outward man, tends to revive the inward man. Is it not so? You may water your pillow with your tears all night, while others are asleep, but that very experience is renewing your soul, strengthening your faith, deepening your love to Christ. Some of you may say, 'I cannot understand that,' but there are others of you, I suppose, who may know this far better than I do. Seek light on the matter from the Scriptures and see if you can find mention of any of the Lord's people who have not experienced these trials. Why then did God send them to them? Was it not that His purpose might be accomplished in them? The Psalmist found that his outward man was failing, but he found great support in the thought: 'Whom have I in heaven but thee? and there is none upon earth that I desire beside thee.' And then he added; 'My flesh and my heart faileth: but God is the strength – the rock – of my heart, and my portion for ever' (*Psa.* 73: 25–26). A man's heart and flesh failing because of his affliction, yet he is able to say 'God is the strength of my heart and my portion for ever.' And that is exactly what I am trying to say!

Another thing I must say although I have often brought it before you. Somehow or other there is something in us constitutionally causing us to require the rod of God upon our backs to keep us right. In what I am about to say, I am including myself as well as you; and I include members of this church even if it were twenty or a hundred times its present size. If my voice could reach them, I would include every one of them. The fact is that if we get on in this world, in our employment, in our family life, in our education; if we get the good things of life, the luxuries, we are liable to forget God. It is indisputably so! It requires the strokes of God to be upon us to make us holy and humble. I do not intend to reason or to argue, but I can say this, and I appeal to the experience of every Christian person here present before me: Is it not the case that when things were really bad with you, when God chastened you, that you prayed more earnestly and thought more of Him in one week than you did in a whole year before then? Of course it is! We never pray more often or earnestly until we are put into the den of lions, into the furnace of fire. Then we do it.

4. *Another thing about the afflictions of Christians is that they are light*

Here we meet with a paradox, for the Word says, 'our light afflictions'. The Apostle's afflictions were not light, they were very heavy, but he calls them light. Let us apply the word to ourselves. First, our afflictions are light in comparison with what we deserve. Yet people often say, 'Nobody in the world has such hard trials as we have.' That is a wrong remark, for our 'light affliction' in comparison with what we deserve is very light. If our Lord were to mark iniquity, 'O Lord, who would stand?' If God were to give you what you deserve, what would happen to you? But He does not. I agree that some people pass through great troubles, through terrible mental depression, or through trials resulting from the illness of relations. Some have to nurse their relations for years and years. These are only examples of the many things I could mention. But at their worst, the Christian's trials are light because – and I want you to notice this in particular – if you are a Christian your afflictions are never the result of divine anger. Never! Affliction is always an exercise of love, never of anger.

Believe, then, that when affliction reaches you, you are suffering under the hand of God. You may say, 'What is going to happen to me? Am I about to be disgraced? Shall I break under this burden?' I answer, You are in the hands of God. You have to regard whatever happens as a loving act from your Father in heaven. If you are a true Christian, God will never punish you in anger. God will never punish you at all. He is chastening you. 'What son is he whom the father chasteneth not?' Whom God loves he chastens. Chastening is always an act of the divine love. So when these trials reach you, and when you go through them, say to yourself, by faith, 'This is the work of the God who loves me. He would not chasten if he did not love me.' That is the way to look at it if you are a Christian. Of course, if you are not a Christian you have no right to look at it like that. Trials reaching the unbeliever contain a message for him of a different kind. They say, 'Seek ye the Lord while he may be found, call ye upon him while he is near . . . he will have mercy . . . he will abundantly pardon' (Isa. 55:6-7).

Let us turn to think of the affliction that came upon our Lord. There is a statement that is occasionally heard but which should never be used. It runs, 'My sufferings are very little in comparison with the sufferings of Christ for me'. The parallel is a wrong comparison. We are using the sufferings of our Lord in an entirely wrong way, if we say that. What do we mean by the sufferings of our Lord? His bodily sufferings? No, we must not think of them in that way. The sufferings known by our Lord were suffering resulting from imputation. But our sufferings are personal sufferings and we deserve them all. His sufferings were those of an innocent person, who had never sinned, but to Him the sins of God's elect were imputed and He suffered for them. So there is no comparison between our sufferings and His; no parallel should be drawn. But when we come to think of what He endured on our behalf, then our afflictions vanish.

Only a few weeks ago, I was reminding my hearers that when Christ was really suffering on the cross, the everlasting arms were not underneath Him, but were bruising Him, crushing Him, smiting Him. It pleased the Lord to bruise Him, and this is what the everlasting arms were doing to Him on the cross, in the darkness. They were bruising Him, but they were not under Him. Think of that! When you are suffering, your afflictions are light, for the everlasting arms are beneath you. They are not smiting you, penally, as they were smiting Christ.

5. But my text says a further thing about these afflictions – they are 'but for a moment'

They are for a moment in comparison with eternal duration. 'A

[88]

moment' Paul calls this lifetime of ours, and soon the day will break and the shadows will flee away. Are you passing through afflictions, brother or sister? Are you in the furnace of fire? Are you in the winepress, feeling that you are being pressed beyond your measure? Are you at home reading the Lamentations of Jeremiah? Is that the way you are? If so, remember that affliction lasts only for a day. 'Sorrow endureth for a night, joy cometh in the morning'. The morning will soon break upon you and the night of darkness and bitterness and tearfulness will be gone. Our 'light affliction' which is but for a moment will soon pass away. You may feel trial to be long; you may wonder many a time whether the day of affliction is ever going to end, and if the light is ever going to shine through the window again. But soon a better light will appear. It will be the light of glory. This is what Paul meant when he said 'our light affliction is but for a moment' – that is to say, a moment in comparison with eternity.

But what is the effect of afflictions on believers now? They 'work a far more exceeding and eternal weight of glory'. I confess that here I come to one of those places in Scripture that I cannot understand or expound. I feel that I am going out into an ocean that is far too deep to be fathomed. Affliction works for us 'a far more exceeding and eternal weight of glory'. The glory that you get out of it, the joy even in this life, the joy of being afflicted in this world, far exceeds the bitterness of the affliction itself. The balm that the Lord supplies far exceeds the pains of His treatment. It is possible for believers to experience the sharpest of afflictions and yet be as composed, as calm and as happy, because of communion with God as ever they were in their lives.

Paul had such an experience. It worked for him 'a far more exceeding and eternal weight of glory'. Words fail to express what he had in mind. Examine the terms that are used. The words in English and in the original never could convey what he had in mind – a 'far more exceeding and eternal weight of glory'. The phrase is a superlative phrase, as if Paul were quite unable to find words to express himself. The Apostle here tells us what afflictions do for Christians, not because they have any merit in themselves, not because of the intensity of them, not because of the number of them, but because they woo us from the world, and they bring us to God. Let me give you one example. When the people of Israel were in the land of Egypt many of them became idolators. Some of them began to worship Egyptian gods. But God led them out of Egypt by the hand of Moses, into the wilderness. There, for forty years, they were secretly and publicly practising idolatry. Finally they took possession of the land of Canaan and for hundreds of years they practised idolatry. Plagues, trials, wars, and the punishment from God did not divorce them from their idols. Then the day came, when the armies of the aliens came against Jerusalem and they burned it with fire, level to the ground. The people of Israel were taken to Babylon and they were there for seventy years. At the end of that time some of them returned to their own land. But my point is, that from the day of their return the Jews were never idolators. The captivity cured them of idolatry.

And in our day, when God sends afflictions upon us He does so to cure us of an illness that is in our heart. He intends to cure us and to make our soul like a weaned child, a child weaned, wanting the mother's breast, the mother's milk, crying after it, and refused it altogether, until at last he becomes contented. 'Surely I have behaved and quieted myself, as a child that is weaned of his mother? my soul is even as a weaned child' (*Psa. 131:2*).

II THE BELIEVER LOOKING AT THINGS UNSEEN

But you may say to me: What is the condition of mind that will make afflictions work for me in this way? In answer, I call you attention to further words of the Apostle: 'We look not at the things which are seen but at the things which are not seen'. Is not this a strange statement? How can a man talk about 'looking not' at things that are seen – what sort of talk is that? It is precisely the same thing that the writer to the Hebrews says about Moses. What enabled him to endure? What enabled him to continue in spite of all his difficulties, for the people threatened to stone him? What was the secret of it? 'He endured, as seeing Him who is invisible' (*Heb. 11:27*). 'We look not at the things which are seen but at the things which are not seen.' Here then are people who look at things which are not seen.

What are the things which are seen? I answer: your afflictions, in all their bearings on your circumstances. You may lose your husband. You say, What am I going to do without him? There could be some selfishness in that, but it is a natural thing to say and we say it. You look at your circumstances and you say 'What am I going to do?' Many a widower says, How am I to live? How am I to look after the children? In various ways we are all prone to look at things seen and to do so in ways which are not Christian. The things which are not seen include an interest in Christ; it is a thing not seen. Some of you may have money in a bank and you have a little book to assure you that it is there. At the same time, however, your name and the amount you have in the bank are entered into a ledger. I know little about these things, but I assume that this is what happens: your name and the amount you have in the bank are recorded in a ledger. But you never see that ledger. Do you believe it is there? If you do, then you are looking at something you do not see, and that you will never see. Apply this to things spiritual when things go against you, look by faith at your interest in Christ. You will never see the Book of Life, but look at it by faith. 'We look not at the things which are seen, but at the things which are not seen.'

Furthermore, among the things which are not seen are the promises of God. They are in the Bible but you fail to see them in the truest sense of all until you are tried and enabled to rest your soul upon them. Among other things God says to you in a time of affliction is, 'I will never leave you nor forsake you'. When you look at that and believe God, you are looking at things which are not seen. I repeat the precious words, 'I will never leave you, and I will never, never forsake you'. You look at the promise and you believe it, and it becomes real to you as your own heart receives its comfort. Paul experienced this joy. He took to heart the divine promises – they are many – and so he went on in the strength of the Lord. Peace, joy, rest, and fulness come from a belief in the promises.

My closing word refers to 'an eternal weight of glory'. He might have said 'a weight of glory'; he speaks of 'an eternal weight (or worth) of glory'. Is not any affliction worth enduring for the little time we are in this world, if we have an eternal weight of glory in prospect? But I must speak a word to those who are out of Christ. What about you? Does the word 'eternal' frighten you? You are on the way to a place that is eternal, and eternity is not time without end. Eternity is timelessness. In the Book of Revelation an angel swears by Him who liveth for ever and ever that there would be time no longer. Do you believe this? Are you troubled at the thought of an eternal weight of woe which is the unbeliever's portion? Naked you came into this world and naked you will leave it. It is pleasant to be rich, it is good to be happy, but I am asking you what will be your lot when you go into this timelessness? Is anything working an eternal weight of glory for you? What a vast difference there is between you and the Christian! God knows I am sorry with all my heart for people who live on earth, and suffer and die and have no Christ, because I know what will happen to them. Everything is working for them an eternal weight of woe. Which then is your portion?

❦ 10 ❦

Constrained by Love

For the love of Christ constraineth us; because we thus judge, that if one died for all, then were all dead. And that he died for all, that they which live should not henceforth live unto themselves, but unto him which died for them, and rose again.

2 Corinthians 5:14, 15[1]

These verses are the keynote to Paul's life of holy devotion and service. If you wish to know what was the mainspring of his life and what kept him going from the day he was converted until the day he died, we have the answer in these verses. He felt in his heart that which carried him on irresistibly against all odds, that made him determined to persevere to the end in spite of difficulties, and here we find it explained: 'the love of Christ constrains us'. Now without that same experience, your life and my life will be absolutely joyless, irrespective of what profession we make and of what we do. If our heart is like a stone, if we do not feel the constraining power of the love of Christ, even though we speak with the tongues of men and of angels and have faith to remove mountains and to give our bodies to be burned, it all amounts to nothing.

I ask then, What is your own experience in this respect? What moves you to lead the Christian life, if you do lead such a life? Is it the constraining power of the love of Christ? Is this the daily experience of your life? If all that you have as a Christian is the interest you had when you were converted many years ago, then you have very little. A child has no consciousness of being born, though he knows it to be a fact; but if he had remained at that stage and made no progress he would be a pitiable specimen of

[1]March 23, 1975.

[93]

humanity. And if you have nothing but the experience of your conversion you are a pitiable Christian. Paul does not say, 'the love of Christ *constrained* me', referring to an experience long past, but he says 'the love of Christ *constraineth* me'. The love that constrained you long ago continues to constrain you to the end of your life. This is real Christianity. So let us ask ourselves as we go on what the love of Christ means to us. Is it merely an abstract concept, or is it something real and felt? Does it move us to obey the Lord in all things? Is it a love that lays hold upon us with irresistible force and that causes us to obey the Lord wholeheartedly? If not, *the* vital thing is missing from our lives. Let us then spend a little time thinking of this constraining power.

'The love of Christ constraineth us'. The love that is in Christ and in believers is a mutual love. Christ loves believers and they love Christ. But what is referred to here is Christ's love to Paul and to all believers. It is that love that constrained him. It is very important for us to notice this. Many people think that it is essential for them to feel their own love to Christ constraining them to Christian service and they believe that this is the most important thing in the Christian life. It is not so! The most important thing in the Christian life is to be conscious of the love that Christ has for you and that is what Paul refers to here.

The love of Christ to Paul was manifested in different ways but supremely by one specific, divine – human act, namely, that Jesus Christ died for him. The death of Christ on Paul's behalf was that which he ever remembered and it was this that spurred him on in Christian service. He never forgot it and it was ever present with him. How often do we think of Christ and His love in the course of a day? That love is the mainspring of a Christian's life. If the mainspring is always wound, as it was in Paul's case, then the constraining love of Christ will compel us to act in a holy way. I do not propose at the moment to speak at length of the love of Christ to believers, of the eternity of that love, of the immensity of it, of its boundlessness, of its continuity, and of all that is included in the love of Christ even unto death and that the death of the cross. Paul was very well aware of all these things. But my present point of all is that the love of Christ was the dynamo that never rested in his soul and that kept his energies working at full speed for his Lord and Master. He never doubted for a single moment that Christ 'died for all', and for himself. He knew that he did not deserve to be loved. The amazing fact that Christ became his substitute and redeemed him from his sin by dying in his stead overwhelmed him. He had to get vent for his feelings and he did so by devoting his life to God in the service of the gospel. Necessity was laid upon him. As he expresses it in another place: 'Yea, woe is unto me if I preach not the gospel'. Thus was the power of Christ's love felt and experienced by Paul.

And now, how do we ourselves respond to the love of Christ? I hope we will not decline in our religion to the extent that we shall think of it merely as a source of enjoyment and no more, 'Did you enjoy the Communion?' someone asks. 'Oh, it was very nice!' God have mercy upon us if that is as far as we go! We should go much further than that! But this is as far as many people go, with regard to our church service. They say, 'Oh, it was nice, it was good, I thoroughly enjoyed it'. I fear the plain fact is that we are not capable of enjoying anything as much as Paul enjoyed the love of Christ in his own soul. What rapturous joy that man had in the love of Christ and by reason of the fact that Christ loved him and died for him. But he did not stop there. He wanted others to become acquainted with his Saviour and Lord. He desired to preach the gospel far and wide and he gave his life to this end. He wished to share his blessings. Did he lose anything by this? Not at all!

The love of Christ and the experience of it is quite different from anything else of which you can think. If you had money and began to share it with other people, the less you would have for yourself. If you had furniture and you began to give it away, the less you would have in your house. But this does not hold true of heavenly things. The more you share the love of Christ with other people the more of it you get for yourself; the more that love flows out from you, the more it flows into you. And Paul was filled with the love of Christ right up to the end of his days, because he shared so much with others. Christ died for all and he rose again. Paul lived to preach this message and the more he did so the more he was enabled to glory in Christ's death. The love of Christ was to Paul a powerful river that could not be dammed up; it had to make a way for itself. And in your life and mine, the same thing must happen. The things that dam this river in our lives from flowing out to others must all be removed so that the waters may swell and run out into a needy world. 'The love of Christ constraineth us'. Notice also that this constraint within the Apostle was the result of a judgment or a conclusion that he had reached. Paul was a thoughtful man and this is one of his conclusions, 'that if one died for all, then were all dead.' And if Christ died for all, he died so 'that they which live should not henceforth live unto themselves but unto him which died for them and rose again'.

In my text Paul does not refer so much to the fact of Christ becoming our Substitute to perform a work of redemption but rather to the fact that He died in order to effect our sanctification and usefulness. Paul does not say that He died to take away our sins, although that is true, and he often refers to it, but his point here is a different one. He tells us here that Christ died so that we might 'live unto Him'. He also says that because Christ died for all, it follows that all His people die to sin in His death. Do you see the point? You died in His death. I ask you to give special heed to what I am about to say. When you die you will do nothing for yourself anymore; your work will be finished. Now, Christian, you who sat at the Lord's Table last Sabbath, you have died; you died in Christ (that is what Paul means) and therefore, being dead, you cannot live for yourself anymore. But in a spiritual sense, although you cannot live for yourself anymore, you can live for *Him*. 'So that henceforth we should not live to ourselves, but unto him who died for us and rose again': note the delightful way in which Paul works out his argument.

This, then, is the constraining motive in all Christians, this love that Christ has to them. Think for a moment of what you were before Christ's love and power laid hold of you. Must you not say: 'I am a man who has sinned against God, and by sinning against God I am exposed to His wrath and curse forever. There is no way out; I must drink that curse by suffering the torments of eternity. But Christ died for me, and if He died for me, a hell-deserving sinner, if He brought me nigh to Him who was so far away from Him, if He made me to feel His love, who had felt nothing but enmity towards Him, I do not intend to live for myself anymore, but to live for Him. I can never pay the debt that I owe to Him.'

Of course you cannot pay that debt! But you can do a little. You can do as much as possible. You can render service according to your capacity and according to your opportunities. You can do as much as that. The Holy Ghost will be your helper. You live by the power of the Holy Ghost, and that power will be given you day by day. And not only so: They who live, live in communion with their

Lord. The Apostle Paul's meaning includes their living in communion with Christ. How do you live physically? By eating once a month? That is not the way to live. There is no healthy man who does not eat every day and when you eat you have communion with your food. The food becomes part of you. And on the spiritual plane, if you live for Christ, you live not on something that you got twenty years ago at your conversion; you live by Christ's communion with you, by Christ becoming a part of you, by communion everyday. Surely you cannot be 'living' if you are out of communion with Christ for such living is like that of the beasts that perish. But a man lives differently, and a Christian lives differently from an unsaved man. He lives by communion with Christ, and so he does not live unto himself anymore.

Do you know what is the greatest temptation a Christian has in this world? It is to live unto himself. And this is what the constraining power of Christ will compel you not to do, and enable you not to do. And He will see to it that you will not do it. It is what Thomas Chalmers called 'the expulsive power of a new affection'. We all live unto ourselves, until the power of Christ's love comes into our hearts. The power that makes us live unto ourselves is ousted and a new power comes in. Self then becomes loathsome to us, and Christ becomes exceedingly precious, immeasurably precious, to our hearts. We no longer live unto ourselves for gain, fame, pleasure, or success. It does not matter one iota what position we fill in this world. It does not matter whether we work at emptying the bins into the dustcart, or are the highest ranking official in an honourable profession. It makes no difference whatsoever to the Christian, whether he is at the bottom of the ladder or at the top. It is what a person *is* that matters. That is what makes all the difference. To be constrained by the love of Christ is all-important. To be poor or well-off in the world has no importance at all.

If a man, the God-man, went up to the cross of Calvary and died for me, to save me from going to hell for ever and to redeem me from sin in this world, surely I must be concerned to know how I can serve Him. Am I not to live for Him? When I think of the Huguenots and the Covenanters I cannot but realize that they were not called on to live for Him – they did that – but they were called on to die for Him. Not in the way in which He had died for them, but out of loyalty to Him and His cause. Very many Christians have died for Christ. When John was on the Isle of Patmos, he saw by specific revelation, the souls of them who were beheaded for the testimony of the Lord Jesus. They seemed to have a special place in heaven. As for ourselves, we have been asked to die for Christ but we are asked to live for Him, to live for Him alone, to live for Him earnestly, constantly, and enduringly; not to live for Him today, or tomorrow, or on the Sabbath merely, but to live for Him without any intermission, to live constantly unto Him; in walk, in thought, to live unto Him. And this is what we can do under the constraining love of Christ in our hearts.

If you went into a house, and discovered that there was a domestic trouble of a very intense kind; if, say, somebody had called in an hour before you went in, and had brought news that a son or a daughter of the home was exceedingly ill, had been run down by a car, was in the intensive care unit in a hospital, and was probably paralysed for life, do you think you would be in that house long before hearing about it? I do not think it would be so. Why? Because there is a power in the heart. The power of love would be working in their hearts, a loved one was in trouble. If you came to that home with a little bit of gossip or day-to-day talk, they would have no interest whatsoever in it, none at all, because there was something else too near their heart – the trouble into which their loved one had fallen. And this was the way it was with Paul. The love of Christ was in his heart, compelling him to speak. It was like a rope pulling him, like a chain drawing him on to live for his Lord and Master.

You may be complaining of the coldness of your heart and the lack of fervency in your prayers and the religious monotony of it all; or that our church services are a little bit too long. You may start yawning during the service, when Christ is preached to you, as some people do. There is a remedy. If you want your coldness taken away, it can be taken away by the fire of the love of Christ burning in your heart. If you desire that religion and sermons about Christ should not be monotonous, then let your heart be filled with love, the love of Christ, and then you will be all ears and all eyes to hear every word about Him. This was the secret of Paul's devotion. And he was not alone. Time compels me to stop. The love that was such a dynamic in his own heart was kindled by his knowledge that Christ loved him and died for him. The two fires burned at one and the same time, the fire of the love of Christ to

Paul and Paul's consciousness of it, and the fire of his love to Christ which was the response to the other and was kindled by it.

Let me give you an illustration of my meaning. You take up your newspaper and may read of a house on fire and of a mother, a poor fragile woman, being restrained by the police and the firemen from entering into the burning building to get her child out of it. What does she care for her body? Why does she rush into a burning building? Is that insanity? Not at all! It is the power of love. She cannot help it, something is pulling her – the love of her child, her compassion is urging her on. And so it was with Paul! Christ's love kindled a love in his heart for the people of God and in this he was not alone. If it was fitting to talk to you just now of the history of the church, I would talk to you of Calvin and Luther, of Knox, Whitefield, Spurgeon and others. I would talk also of such women as Mary Slessor of Calabar and Amy Carmichael. What kept them going? Difficulties there were of numerous kinds; sometimes their lives were threatened; sometimes their houses were burned over their heads. What kept them going? The love of Christ! The love of Christ! 'The love of Christ constraineth us'. Because One died for all, then we are all dead so that we who live in Christ, and in union and communion with Him, should not henceforth live unto ourselves nor unto the world which is going to perish.

We are only here for a little time. We are not called to live for money or pleasure or success or fame or anything like that, but to live unto Christ and for Christ. And we purpose to tell all those around us that Jesus died to save sinners, rose again, having finished the work that the Father gave Him to do. I ask you, then, as I close, How do you stand now? I know very well that my words will be of no use of themselves. Apart from divine grace, I know that all I have said is not going to make a particle of difference to those who are dead in soul. Some of you who are listening to me will carry on in the same old way, and will do so until the Spirit of God rouses you, if He will, from your sleep, and from your death in trespasses and sins. If in His mercy He does so, He will soak you in the love of Christ. All things will have passed away and all things will become new. May that happen to us all!

∞ II ∞

Feasting with Christ

He brought me to the banqueting house, and his banner over me was love.
Song of Solomon 2:4[1]

There are different kinds of sermons, and as I have often said to my congregations, the preacher of the gospel must always strike a balance and not be one-sided. There are sermons that deal especially with doctrine. We find this particularly in the Epistle to the Romans. There are also experimental sermons and if you want to get an example of these read the Book of Psalms. Then, too, there are practical sermons. These you will find scattered throughout the Epistles.

The text before us is an experimental text and I intend to speak on it from that point of view. When we speak about an experimental text and preach an experimental sermon we do not expect everyone in the congregation to be able to follow it, because there are those who know little about experience. But I believe that there are some in this congregation who will know in their own experience what the church of Christ actually means when she says that Christ brought her to the banqueting house and that His banner over her was love.

We note at the outset that this is a love-song between Christ and the church. Sometimes Christ speaks of and to the church; at other times the church speaks to Him and tells about Him, and it is the church who speaks here, saying, 'He brought me to the banqueting house'.

I THE PLACE TO WHICH THE CHURCH WAS BROUGHT

Christ's bride calls it 'the banqueting house'. Obviously it includes

[1]June 27, 1976.

[100]

the meaning that if He brought her to it then she was not always there. If a man is brought to a house it is because he was not always in the house. And that is true in this case as in all other cases. Without reference just now to the sinful alienation between Christ and the unregenerate soul, there are times when true Christians are not in the banqueting house of Christ, and yet they are as truly Christian as those who are in the house. But they are just not feasting with Christ. As there is a time of feasting in the Christian life, so there is a time of fasting. Our text implies that the church is not always in the banqueting house.

Our text also refers to the priceless ordinances of the gospel which we possess, and here we are being taught to know what these are. They include, to state them very briefly:

1. The preaching of the Word

What would we do for our souls without the preaching of the gospel? Would the Word and the Sabbath Day be enough? No! If that were enough then the Lord would not have established preaching. But the Lord appointed preaching because it was meant to be a banqueting house for His people – a place where their souls would be fed. You Christian people who are here today, and who have been listening to my ministry for so long, if your souls are not fed – not by me but by the preaching that I give – then it is a fearful reflection both upon the preaching and upon myself. Preaching ought to be to your souls like a banquet to the hungry. No man should ever come inside a church without feeling the better for it inwardly. And if it is not so, there is something wrong. I am not saying that it is wrong with you, for it may be the ministry that is at fault. It cannot be wrong with the Bible or with the text, but the wrong may be with the minister.

There is nothing more pathetic than a soul famishing in the presence of food. You know what difficulty doctors have in this very matter, when they come across a person who has no appetite whatsoever for food. The food is there but the person has no appetite. The doctors do their best by their medicine and by their coaxing to make him eat, but to no avail. Well now, if it is the case that we have no appetite for the food which God provides in the preaching of the gospel, there is something wrong with the preaching. I maintain this very strongly. You think of all the types of experiences that are present here even in one day. There are people who are very happy – young married couples; people who are getting on well in the world. There are people who are sad – people who have recently been bereaved; people who feel something wrong with themselves physically; people who are depressed mentally. There are all sorts of experiences, and the point I make is, that unless the preaching of the gospel meets your need and helps you, and is a banquet to you in your circumstances, then there is something very far wrong.

2. Again there is the banqueting house of prayer

Prayer is a marvellous thing. We would die if we could not pray. But prayer is a wonderful avenue by which we draw nigh unto God. It is a private access to the palace of the King. Try to get into Buckingham Palace without a warrant and see what will happen to you. There are guards clicking their heels; there are men at the gate, and they will not let you in unless you have a warrant. But the point about prayer is that we always have a warrant and there are no guards to keep us out from the presence of the King. And when we come into the presence of the King it is a banquet to our souls. I never said to anyone – and I never will – 'stop praying'; but I say this – and I shall always say it – that if our prayers are formal, if they go unanswered, and if they mean nothing more than that we bend our knees and address some invisible person for a little while, then there is something wrong with our prayers. Remember that in prayer God Himself is speaking to you as you also are speaking to God. And when you pray aright you get into the banqueting house because there God feeds your soul.

3. Then, of course, there is the Word – the Bible

The Bible is inestimably precious and what a banqueting house it is! What would you do if things went against you, say in your family life, or in your professional life, or in your physical life? What would you really do? Would you try to get comfort by telling your woes to a friend or going to the doctor? These certainly have their uses as far as they go. But what I suppose you would really do is go to the Bible, and before long you would come across

something in the Bible that would meet your need and prove a
banquet to your soul.

4. And then, there are the sacraments

I firmly believe that there are Christian men and women here today
who were converted long ago and yet they have never sat at the
table of the Lord. Whatever else may be said to them, this can be
said to them: you are missing a feast, a banquet in which you would
otherwise take part if you were obedient. By not coming, they are
missing a meal that would satisfy their souls, and they therefore
ought to be there. So much, then, about what is meant by the
house!

But I must also tell you that there is only one door leading into it.
You cannot get in, in any way you like. The door is the door of
regeneration or the door of saving grace. Jesus said, 'I am the
door', and there is no way whatsoever into communion with God
but through Jesus Christ. You cannot get into a communion by the
mere exercise of your own emotions; you cannot organize a series
of meetings and have a wonderful time and think that is
communion. No! Communion is a thing by itself. And it is only
through Christ that communion is had with the Father, and
through the Spirit that communion is had with Himself. That is
the only door. If you try to get in by any other way you will fail, but
if you seek it through Christ you will win.

The house is founded upon a Rock and is therefore perfectly
safe. I would like to emphasize that point. The ordinances of the
gospel are safe for our souls, but nothing else is safe. Even if you
saw a vision of angels, that would be no token that you are a saved
soul. Even if you heard a voice from heaven with your natural ears,
that would not be a sure token that you are a child of God. But if
you make use of the gospel ordinances and trust in the promises of
the Word, then that is a sign, and a sure sign, that you are a child of
God. This is the only safe house and all the rest are unsafe.
Furthermore, it is roofed with the blood of Christ. No drop of
wrath will ever seep through it, for the blood is over it. And then
again, Jesus Himself is always present in it. Whoever else may be
absent from His banqueting house, He is always there. A marriage
is not a marriage if there is no bridegroom. He is the Bridegroom
and the church is His bride, and where the one is, there is also the

other. And last of all, regarding the house, believers are always welcome into it. If they come they will never be turned away.

Let me just draw a picture for a moment of the way some people talk. They tell you, 'Oh, I am poor and ragged and unworthy to sit at the Lord's table; I am unworthy to pray. I am not like the rest of the Lord's people; I am just like the tail-end; I feel there is something missing'. I would remind such persons of the story of that poor young man who left the far country and came ragged and filthy – just as he was – to his father's home. The father ran to embrace him and told the servants to clothe and feed him. And this is the way it is. Whatever you feel like today as a Christian, even if you feel yourself the worst and the vilest of the vile, come just as you are and I tell you on the warrant of heaven by my God that you will not be turned away. 'Whosoever cometh unto me I will in no wise cast out'. It does not matter what we are like. O my friends, I can give my testimony just as Samuel Rutherford did in a verse which I am going to quote in a moment. If I stood on my own merit I would never have had a moment of communion with Christ in the past, nor would I ever hope to have it in the future. But I do not stand upon my own merit but upon the merits of Christ.

II THE ONE WHO BRINGS THE CHURCH THERE

Who brings whom to the banqueting house? The church says: '*He*,' that is, Jesus Christ Himself, 'brought me' – He because none else but He can do it. Look at the matter in the following way. At times when you come to church you may like my sermons and you feel that I am speaking directly to yourself and to your case; at other times I preach but your mind wanders and I just have nothing whatsoever for you at all. You get bored and uninterested and you long to get out. That is the way with us all. But why is it so if we are Christians? For this reason: that if the holiest man who ever was, and the best preacher who ever was, stood in this pulpit, he could not take you to the banqueting house by any power in himself. The preacher cannot make the Word effectual to you and he cannot give the unction of the Spirit. God alone can do that. And at this point I think it is good to give true believers an encouraging sign: if you are able to get communion with God at any time you please, and if you are easily

[104]

moved in religious services, I would begin to doubt that you have very much good in you, or indeed any good at all. But if you are one of the people who strive after and who long to get communion with God, and who cannot get it, nor see any means of finding it, then that shows that you know something of Christ. You want that which neither yourself nor anyone else can give to you. I confess that is the kind of person I like and that is the kind of person I would like to be. But remember, I do not mean people who *say* that they would like to get communion with God and then forget Him all day long, for that sort of thing is hypocrisy of the worst kind.

Notice further, that the bringing is an act of condescending grace. 'He brought me to the banqueting house'. I am reminded of the story of King David and Mephibosheth who was lame in both his feet. Mephibosheth called himself a dead dog and he could not have abased himself more. But the King told him, 'Mephibosheth, it is my will that you sit at my table for ever after, and your place will be with me, the King'. Although Mephibosheth may have felt as a dead dog it made no difference to David; he was doing it for Jonathan's sake and Mephibosheth retained that privilege for the rest of his life. What an act of condescension that was on the part of David! O my friend, when you think of what *you* are; when you call to mind all your sins, your rebellion, your prayerlessness, your distracted thoughts; when you come to think of your own utter uselessness, and, then, that, in spite of it all, God grants you communion with Christ, is not that an act of unspeakable, condescending grace? Such is the thought of that beautiful verse in Mrs. Cousin's poem based on Samuel Rutherford's sayings:

> *Oh! I am my Beloved's,*
> *And my Beloved's mine!*
> *He brings a poor vile sinner*
> *Into His 'house of wine'.*
> *I stand upon His merit*
> *I know no other stand,*
> *Not e'en where glory dwelleth*
> *In Immanuel's land.*

Not even in heaven, let alone on earth, is there any other way whereby He brings a poor vile sinner into His house of wine.

III HOW HE BRINGS THE CHURCH THERE

How does the Lord bring them in?
There are certain preparations to be made before He brings them in. I mention two or three of them, very briefly.

1. *He washes them in His own blood*

Friend, whosoever you are, be certain of this: You cannot get in without this washing. You must be washed, for His eye will not behold iniquity in anyone. If you try to get communion with God, and say that you get it and yet 'walk in darkness,' you lie and do not tell the truth (*1 John 1:6*). Notice the Scriptures do not say that you must be perfect before you can have communion with God. What they say is that you must be washed in the blood of Christ from all your sins. You must be justified and regenerated.

2. *You must be clothed in the righteousness of Christ*

Remember how, in the parable, one man tried to get in without the wedding garment, but he did not get away with it. When the King came in to inspect the guests He said to this man: 'Friend, how did you come hither without the wedding garment?' (*Matt. 22:12*) And the King told the servants to take the speechless man, to bind him hand and foot, and to cast him into outer darkness, where the wicked are. Ah, my friend, you may deceive yourself and others, but you cannot deceive the King. You must have the robe of the righteousness of Christ upon you before you can get into 'the house of wine'. You cannot get in otherwise; do not deceive yourself into thinking that you can. I say that because I have been convinced during my ministry that there are people who have such low opinions of the gospel that they really believe they are Christians when they are not. People talk to me and tell me, 'Oh! I do my best; I pray and things like that.' But that is not the point at all. That is not Christianity and that is not real religion. Real religion consists in being united to God and in doing what God commands us to do. And this is part of it – to be clothed with the righteousness of Christ – Jehovah Tsidkenu! We must be like Him and conformed to His image.

3. And there is a perfume which you need before you get into 'the house of wine' – a perfume that comes from the love you have to God in your heart

When people – especially the women folk – go to weddings or to any special functions, they usually sprinkle on one kind of perfume or another over their inner garments, and God must smell upon you, as it were, this perfume of love to Himself, because He will not let you into His banqueting house if you do not love Him.

4. And yet again, you get in to 'the house of wine' by the way of obedience

Obedience is not a merit but you cannot get in if you are disobedient. 'If ye be willing and obedient, ye shall eat the good of the land' (*Isa. 1:19*).

IV THE GUESTS WHO WILL BE THERE

Who are the guests who will be there with you? The family of faith, of course! None else! But not all even of them will be there, for in the church of Christ, unfortunately, there are people who are out on the doorstep. If somebody came to the door of this church but did not want to come in, if he put his ear to the key-hole he might hear the sermon but he would lose the atmosphere completely. He would not have the atmosphere of worship which we have here if he did that. The elder brother in the parable would not go in because he grudged his brother the place which his father gave him at the table, and in the church of Christ there are people like the elder son – out on the fringe! And there are other people who, to use an old Highland phrase, are 'far ben'. They get right in to where the Master of the house is – right into His presence. John lay on the bosom of Christ at the Supper. Mary sat at the feet of Christ in the house of Bethany – but Martha did not. And the other disciples did not lie on His bosom as John did. And there are some in the church of Christ just like that.

In this banqueting house there are no grudges one against another. Nobody grudges another his place in the house. This is the difference between natural things and spiritual things. If I am not mistaken, the more we get of temporal things, the more we want them and the more greedy we get. The Bible says that 'he who loves silver shall not be satisfied with silver' (*Eccles. 5:10*). And you may say, and I may say, 'Well, if I had £10,000, I would give so many hundreds to this and to that'. I am not so sure but that you are giving more now than you would give if you had £10,000. And the same is true of me. But that is not the case with spiritual things. The more you get of Christ, the more you want to share Christ.

There is an old story, which I heard often in my young days, of two people who were down by the shore and found a cask washed up by the waves. They took the bung out and tasted it, to discover that it contained well-matured whisky. Well, of course, they decided that they would not share it with anybody; they would hide it in the sand and come now and again with their mugs to get a portion each. But before they went away they had a real, good drink and as drink goes to the head and loosens the tongue, they were so drunk that they went up and down the road, through the village telling everyone to come and taste what they had found. And you see, this is exactly the way with those who taste of the love of Christ for themselves. When you get Christ into your heart, instead of keeping Him to yourself, you want to tell everybody about Him because you want the whole world to share with you what you have found for yourself, and you therefore do not grudge anyone else his place.

What are the viands to be found on the table when He brings you to the banqueting house? Jesus said: 'Except ye eat the flesh of the Son of man, and drink his blood, ye have no life in you' (*John 6:53*) 'My flesh is meat indeed and my blood is drink indeed'. The Jews could not tell what the words meant. But they mean nothing less than this, that the true Christian lives on Jesus Christ every day. It means that He gives you pardon and peace and sufficiency of grace; you rest upon Him and your soul delights in all that He is in His own glorious character and person. It never entered my head that any of you may leave this church today and say 'What a wonderful sermon that was!' I never thought of such a thing, but even if you were to say just that, it would not mean anything at all to me and it would mean even less to you. But if you were to say: 'What a marvellous Saviour we have! how lovely Christ is! there is no Person like Him!. The minister exalted Him and raised Him and adored Him; I never saw anybody like Him and He has just put everything else out of my mind but Himself' – well, that would be feeding upon Christ. When you see the supreme grandeur of His personal character; when He gives you pardon and sufficiency of grace and peace of conscience and the joy of His own conscious presence, and all that could be desired by a poor needy sinner – these things are the viands at the table, the glorious provision. Oh! friends, why do you not come? Why do you stay outside, famishing and dying, when Christ has a table for you where you can get forgiveness of sins? Every sin you ever committed will be wiped out! Why are you sad and worried about things when you can get Christian joy that the world can never take away? Why do you battle alone when there is a sufficiency of grace? Why are you lonely when there is a presence that will never leave you? I often tell that to folk in old people's homes and hospitals. I tell them that there is One who can be with them all the time. Do we know that? The provision is incomparable for abundance and variety and richness.

What do these people do at the banqueting table? What is the theme of their conversation? They are in communion with Christ and in communion with one another. A strange banqueting house it would be if one refused the right hand of fellowship to another. But that does not happen there. And (listen hard, my friends) in Christ's banqueting house there are no cliques. When people get into the banqueting house they do not just select some people to get in and then run away so that other people won't know where they are going. That happens in this world even among so-called Christian people. They want only a select few, their own chief friends; they do not want others and they run away from them. But that does not happen in the banqueting house of Christ. Not at all! When you are having communion with Christ you do not care who comes in, because you want to share your communion. So there is none of that in it.

Furthermore there is no gossip in the banqueting house of Christ. If you are a professing Christian and it is your manner to go into houses and talk to people in order to find out something about others and then to repeat what you have heard, you are certainly not in the banqueting house with Christ. That is not what people do in the banqueting house. They talk about Christ. He is the substance of their conversation and the theme of it and they cannot do anything else but talk about Him, and speak of Him. You talk about what is nearest your heart. I am quite sure that if you had a son or a daughter put into the grave yesterday and you went into a house, you would care very little what people were talking about. What you would talk about is your grief over your lost child. Think of it in this way: Jesus went to the cross of Calvary for His people and He bled and died. How can we talk of other people and their concerns, and things like that, when this is the case? We shall not do it when we sit in His banqueting house. When we think of the fact that He rose again and now sits at the right hand of the Majesty on high, and that He is coming back to the world, it is a wonder we can talk of anything else!

V THE SIGN OVER THE BANQUETING HOUSE

The last thought I am going to mention is this: What is the sign of the banqueting house, and how do we know it from all other places? Here again let me introduce the subject of Holyrood or Buckingham Palace. If you were to visit Holyrood or Buckingham Palace or Balmoral, or any of the places where the Sovereign is in residence, you would not need to ask anyone whether the Queen was there or not. All you need to do is to look at the flagpole and if the Royal Ensign is flying at top mast, then the Sovereign is in residence, but if the Queen is not in residence then the flag is not there. And here the church says: 'His banner over me was love'. When the King is in residence He raises His own banner, His own ensign. You know how in the flag of Britain we have the emblem of a lion – the flags of other countries have their own emblems – but Christ has the emblem of love. 'His banner over me was love'. Love written in letters of His own blood was the banner He raised over her.

Furthermore it is a banner to engage. The banner is raised to engage people to come in. How then can you stay out? I am telling you today that Christ has a banqueting house and that the banner over it is His own love – the love that brought Him from glory to assume our nature and took Him to the manger and to the ignominy of the cross – and you see it raised in the gospel. How can you stay out? Why do you not come to Him and engage and enlist yourself in His service? 'His banner over me was love'.

And it is a banner to entertain sinners – one to be enjoyed! Why should the church of Christ distress herself so long as she knows that the banner of the love of Christ is hanging over her head? I have every sympathy with you, my friend, because I know that in this world you are full of troubles and of tribulations; you have your own and I have my own; but what is to be our comfort? Is it that some day we shall get rid of them? No! We shall never get rid of them; we shall get rid perhaps of those we have today, but then tomorrow will bring something new. But what of that? If the banner of the love of Christ is over us, all is going to be well. 'His banner over me was love', and this gave the church incredible joy.

And then, it was a banner to bear witness. The church was not ashamed if somebody said to her: 'There is the banqueting house of Christ and there is the banner of Love'. And do you know who is in it? John is there, and Mary is there, and many a poor sinner besides; and are you going to be ashamed when they tell you that you are in the banqueting house with Christ? No, my friends! Let us witness to Him and let us sit under His banner. But I want to plead with you. Whether you are Christian or not, see to it that before the night is out you get into the banqueting house with Christ. And if you get in, you will never want to go out. You will 'go out' in this world and you will have your times of famine and poverty, of coldness and privations, but one day He will take you into the banqueting house above and you will never more go out. Are you, my dear friend, among these people?

❧ 12 ❧

Never Forsaken

I will never leave thee, nor forsake thee.

Hebrews 13:5[1]

The Bible is full of exhortations and directions for the leading of the Christian life. It warns us of our dangers, tells us how to avoid them, and gives us reasons why we should avoid them. One of the greatest of all dangers is that of discontentment. And it is more than a danger: it is the greatest of sins in the eyes of the Lord. It always leads to covetousness, and of all sins there is no sin more abominable in the eyes of the Lord. If there is any sin that offends the Majesty on high it is the sin of covetousness. It consists in wishing that we were something that we are not, in wanting to possess something that we have not, in desiring something that it is not God's will to give us. Stern warnings are given in the Word of God concerning it and Christians ought to be aware of it as much as, if not more than, any other sin. Yet the sad truth is that we can be guilty of it without knowing it. I knew a man who, in the opinion of all who knew him, and not myself only, was covetous. He could not hide it; he was naïve enough, simple enough, for it to come to the surface. And yet, without any hesitation at all, he would wax eloquent on the sin of covetousness. Evidently he did not know that he was guilty and to charge him with the fault would have seemed a tremendous mistake to those who did not know him well.

But is not this the way with us all? Perhaps, concerning ourselves, we hold that we should be thankful to God that of whatever else we may be guilty, we are not guilty of covetousness. Are you quite sure? Sin does not always appear in its true form. When Satan came into Eden he came in as a serpent, and with the

[1]April 23, 1973.

[112]

serpent's guile. And covetousness can put on other garments so that people do not recognize it. It can put on the dress of humility, the dress of contentment, and so we who may be most guilty of it, are perhaps not even aware that it is in us at all. When Paul was converted, this was one of the first things that he saw wrong with himself. He said, 'I had not known lust, except the law had said, Thou shalt not covet' (*Rom. 7:7*). What, then, is the antidote to covetousness? Why should we not covet? Because the Lord hath said, 'I will never leave thee, nor forsake thee'.

I THE PROMISES OF GOD

In its general aspect, not only is my text an antidote to covetousness, but it is one of the sweet promises in the Bible to the child of God. Notice that the writer says, 'Be content with such things as ye have, for he (the Lord) hath said, I will never leave thee, nor forsake thee'. He is quoting the Lord's promise. But where does he find it? He is not quoting exactly anything from the Old Testament with which he was well acquainted. He is not quoting any passage word for word, but he is quoting the substance of what is found in abundance in the Bible. God did not say these exact words but He said the substance of them. And the writer takes the substance of the Scriptures rather than quoting a particular verse. If this is not a lesson for us, I do not know what is. It is especially so for people who talk about 'getting texts' for themselves, or to put it in another way, who talk about texts 'speaking to them', particular texts coming before their mind, and speaking to them. Now, while I am not at all discounting such a method, what really counts when we are profited by the Scriptures, is not necessarily one particular text, but the substance of the Scriptures.

Somebody asked me recently after I recovered my health, what text was made most precious to me when I became sick. I said, I cannot answer that question, for the whole Bible seemed to have been more precious to me when I was sick than before I became ill. I could not say that one text became more precious than any other part of it, although that could have been the case. It is the substance of the Bible, the tenor of the Bible, that really counts. And this is what the writer of Hebrews is telling us. The promises of God are comparable to letters that are delivered to us.

Sometimes, I suppose, every postman, like everyone else, makes a mistake. You go to the door and look at the letters, and you see that one of them is not for you at all; it is addressed to your neighbour, or someone near at hand, but by mistake it was left with you. And there are promises in the Word of God which are not for every Christian, any more than the letter that was left by mistake was for you. Some promises in the Word are made for certain circumstances and occasions, and they are not for us if we are not in those circumstances. 'For thy sake we are killed all the day long; we are accounted as sheep for the slaughter' (*Rom. 8:36*). We could never say that. It is not true of us at all. We have never suffered such persecution as the Apostle mentions. So the promises made for persecuted believers are not meant to be taken by us. Their message is not addressed to us.

Other promises are like circular letters which the postman delivers. He goes about with a bag, especially at General Election times, and there is a letter for every household. The same thing is written in them all. Now what is for all is for the individual as well. We know very well that all these letters have the same words in them, but I get one and you get one, and therefore, although the letter has not been written for us in particular, yet it belongs to us, because our name and address is on it. And that is the way with the promise in our text. It is general and it is for all.

II WHY THE PROMISE WAS GIVEN

Next, let us look to see why the promise was given in the first place. Why is it given at all? Why does the Epistle make it so clear and plain that God says to His own people, 'I will never leave thee, nor forsake thee'. First of all, there is this reason: that sometimes we fear we shall be forsaken. That fear is dishonouring to God. We should not have that fear but we have it all the same. And I suppose when our faith is weak we cannot help having it. To be forsaken is to be left destitute by a friend. Your enemies do not forsake you. But when friends, with whom you may have been very friendly, forsake you, then you are left destitute, and lonely and hopeless. Your state is not an envious one by any means. This, then, is what is meant. God says, 'I will never leave you as your friends may do'. He is so gracious to us, that He answers our childish and dishonouring and unbelievable fears, and condescends to speak to us when we are in troublesome situations, when we are afraid, and He says, 'I will never leave thee, nor forsake thee'.

The people of God in the days of the prophet Isaiah said, 'The Lord hath forsaken me and my Lord hath forgotten me' (*Isa. 49:14*). In one of the Psalms the Psalmist is praying that God would not forsake him, for he feared that it might happen to him. So he made his prayer to God not to forsake him. Similarly, there are certain times in our Christian experience when this fear overcomes us, that God will forsake us. You say, What times are these? First of all, when we are very conscious of inward corruption, then we are afraid that God will forsake us. It is of no use talking to people about a consciousness of their inward corruption unless they know about it. But it can be so severe, so acute, that you feel as if you were an outcast from God and from men; you feel that it is utterly impossible for God and you to be at one any more. You feel a great horror in your soul; 'The pains of hell gat hold upon me', said one, 'I found trouble and sorrow' (*Psa. 116:3*). An agent from hell was burning within him and he could not see how this could be true and yet that God should not forsake him. He was certainly afraid.

Possibly, you are afraid, because of your consciousness of your indwelling sin, that this will happen to you. You feel that you are the greatest sinner in the world. You feel, as it were, like running away from yourself and hiding. You are ashamed to go into the presence of God because of your consciousness of your sin. Even so, God says, 'I will never leave thee, nor forsake thee'. But I want to take the matter further even than that. God gives this promise because sin sometimes prevails against us. Not only are we conscious of its motions within us, but sometimes it gets the better of us and prevails against us, and when it does so, and leaves us in the mire, and makes ruin and havoc of us, then we are afraid that God will forsake us. That experience happened to a better man than you or I. He was a man after God's own heart. One day sin got the better of him, and dragged him into the mire. And what did he then say? You know the familiar words, 'O God, cast me not away from thy presence; and take not thy Holy Spirit from me' (*Psa. 51:11*). That was his reaction. He was oppressed, sin had prevailed over him, and he was afraid that God would leave him destitute, friendless, hopeless, and in despair. These, then, are two reasons for which we are afraid that God will forsake us.

But sometimes the promise is given us because it seems that God has forsaken us. Looking at things on the plane of human reason, it appears as if God has forsaken us. We can fall into thinking that there is no other explanation for our circumstances but that God has forsaken us. In these circumstances God gives this promise to those who seem to be forsaken by Him: 'I will never leave thee, nor forsake thee'. What are these times when we seem to be forsaken? They are times of mysterious providence, the depths of which we cannot fathom. There is a mysteriousness in the providence of God. Take, for example, the case of David. He was anointed to be king over Israel and almost immediately he became a fugitive. The reigning king of Israel sought his life and for years David did not sleep in a bed. He had to live in the mountains and in the dens and caves of the earth. Did it not seem as if God had forsaken him? Events did not suggest the love and compassion, the care and purpose of God. It looked as if God had given David up, but it was not so.

Take an even clearer example of the problem, that of Job. Judging by the eye of human reason, Job's friends said to him, 'God has forsaken you utterly'. That is what it looked like. Apply it to yourself. If God gives you temporal blessings in providence, if He gives you a home or a family, or gives you property, and then you lose all, does it not seem as if God has forsaken you? On one occasion, when I was quite young, I was standing at a church door waiting for someone to go in with me. It was not in my own district. Two men met, who evidently knew each other. They had not met for many a year – probably they had worked together when they were young – and so they greeted one another very warmly. One of the men asked the other about his wife and family. Oh, he replied, I have no wife and family. My wife and my family – nine of them, the whole family – are lying side by side in the cemetery. I never forgot those words and the man's expression as he spoke them. Did it not seem as if God had completely forsaken the man? It is easy enough to speak of faith in days of prosperity, just as anyone can speak of ocean storms when sitting safely at the fireside. It is another thing to be in the storm. It is only when faith is tried in this way that we know whether we have it or not. When the pressures of life come heavily upon us and faith is tried severely, God's utterances are liable to be misjudged, and the soul is apt to say, though it is not the language of faith, 'The Lord hath forsaken me and my Lord hath forgotten me'.

Or take another example: Take extreme poverty like that of Lazarus, the man who lay at the rich man's gate, full of sores (*Luke 16:20*). Picture the scene to yourself. We see a rich man with a beautiful mansion, clothed in purple and fine linen, his table richly laden. He had servants in plenty. Everything that he wanted, he possessed. At his gate, waiting to see if he could get a crumb, was the poor man with open sores which the dogs came to lick. Which of these two men seemed to be the friend of God? The rich man, if your reason speaks, not the poor man! Would God leave a man in the condition of Lazarus if He loved him, lying in the gutter, full of sores, no one going near him, the dogs coming to lick his sores and with little if anything to eat. Think of it. Did it not seem as if God had forsaken Lazarus?

Or consider a different situation. It looks as if God has forsaken His people when He hides His face from them, as He sometimes does. Take the state of the church today. It seems that God has forsaken her. When you read the newspapers and learn what people are saying, the church does not seem to count any more. And if these people mean that she does not count any more in the estimation of men, they are certainly not far wrong. Most certainly she does not count for much today. She has not got the divine power that she used to have. Her work and labours do not meet with the same success as used to be the case. It seems as if God has turned His back upon her. It seems as if God has forsaken the church. And sometimes, to the individual Christian, the darkness is so real, the loneliness so horrifying, that it seems to him that God has turned His back upon him. If you were never in such an experience pray to God that you never will be, because if you are, you will prefer death rather than life. It is a terrible state to be in, but sometimes some souls are put into it and God hides His face from them in their distress. I had a letter the other day from someone I know and I would need a heart of stone not to be affected by it. It told of one sorrow after another, sorrow upon sorrow, a waiting for the comfort that never seemed to come, for an answer from God who never seemed to hear. It is a terrible situation to be in and looking at a case like that, unless you believed the Scriptures you would say that the Lord had forsaken one of His own people. That is what it looked like.

III THE PARTIES TO THE PROMISE

But let me turn to the promise. And there are two parties involved. *'I'* and *'Thee'*. God said, 'I will never leave thee, nor forsake thee'. First I will say a little about the two parties and then move on to the substance of the promises. Who is the 'I'? It is God, infinite and omnipotent, the God whose grace is always all-sufficient, the God for whom nothing is too hard, the loving God who will never cease to love, the unchanging God. All these things and more could be said of the person who speaks the words, 'I will never leave thee, nor forsake thee'. What if anyone else said it? Many a person has said a similar thing to another, and meant it all with all his heart, and later forsaken the object of his love. But God will not change. Many a person in the heat of love has said such things and later his heart has grown cold, the promise has been broken, but God's love never grows cold, and His promise is never forfeited. Think of all that He is. All that He is warrants you to believe that His promise will be fulfilled. If *'he* hath said', you do not need to care what anybody else says to you, and you do not need to care if anybody forsakes you. He hath said, 'I will never leave thee, nor forsake thee'. It would be far better for you to be a Lazarus with not even a crumb or a bed, or hardly enough clothing to cover your body, and the dogs licking your sores, but with the promises of God on your side rather than be the rich man without those promises. There is no comparison at all between the two states.

And now a word about the other party to the promise: *'Thee'*. 'I will never leave *thee'*. The word is in the singular, not in the plural. God speaks to every individual in His church – I will never leave you. Now look at the promise itself. First of all, you do not deserve it. For many reasons you do not deserve that God should say that to you. But I will only mention one. It is the fact that you often forsake God. If there is any one sin of which you and I are guilty it is the sin of infidelity towards our God. Peter knew in his heart what it was to deny the Saviour. And, have not we proved unfaithful also? Oh, shame upon us, for our unfaithfulness and our infidelity towards God! It is one of our blackest sins; it is engrained in our nature; it is a sin of scarlet, of crimson; we have been so unfaithful to God. We have been unfaithful to Him today since we left our beds. If we look back on the past week, we find it to be a record of unfaithfulness to God. For my own part, though I like a searching sermon, and to review my life in order to lay it before my God and ask His forgiveness from His wrath, sometimes I am afraid to do it because my unfaithfulness stands out against me like the sun shining in the noonday sky. A terrible thing is unfaithfulness to God. And yet it is to the unfaithful that God says, 'I will never leave you'.

Perhaps tonight your conscience is smiting you. You say: 'I did not speak for Him when I could have done and should have done so. I did not serve Him when I had the opportunity. I was not prayerful when I had plenty of time to pray.' I know all such feelings. Yet I ask, What does God say? He says to us, 'I will never leave you, although you have often left Me'. There is a sorrowing for us. As we do not deserve His forgiveness, it must be given us for the sake of Jesus Christ, our Lord, for the sake of the merit of His death, and His intercession. God who is sovereign gives it, God in the freedom of His grace gives it. We do not deserve it. We must never think that we can work ourselves up to a pitch and get ourselves into a state where we can deserve God's presence and companionship. That can never be. God gives us His promise only on the grounds of His Son's merit, and of His Son's intercession, which will always prevail. When you remember then, that God says to His own people – 'I will never leave *thee*, nor forsake thee', think of Jesus Christ the Lord and give Him the glory. It is a comfortable promise, for there is nothing the believer dreads in this life more than that God will forsake him.

Sometimes you hear people telling of their fears that this will happen and that will happen. We ought to be ashamed of ourselves as Christian people when we talk like that. The truth is, that it does not matter what happens, as long as God does not forsake us. What if we lose everything? Job lost everything; what of it! If God does not forsake us, the loss of all does not matter. The promise before us is a comforting promise. If you dread that one day you will be left without your God, that day will never come. And it is not only a comforting promise, it is also a suitable promise. Suitable for every occasion! Suitable for every class of person, for ministers and elders; suitable for old and young; suitable for rich and poor; indeed it is suitable for all; as suitable for you as it is for me. And I thank God that it is as suitable for me as it is for you. There is nothing that we ought to be more sure of tonight than this, that the promise of God is 'I will never leave you'. It is as suitable for you as

God could make it. It is tailor-made, so to speak. It was tailor-made in heaven. It was fashioned there in the eternal covenant, precisely to fit your need. Do not think that there can be anything wrong with it. Do not think that a stitch in the promise will ever be loose; do not think that there will be a misfit at any time. It does not matter how much you grow; the suit will always fit you. The dress will always be your measure: 'I will never leave thee, nor forsake thee'.

IV THE CERTAINTY OF THE PROMISE

Now notice that this is an emphatic promise. The fact is that we do not read it aright. Do you know how many times the word 'never' is in the original text? In our translation it is found once only, but in the original it occurs five times. Very often, in languages like the Greek, two negatives were used to make a positive, to make a positive statement more positive. Here we have five negatives together, literally, 'For he hath said, I will never, never, never leave thee, and I will never, never forsake thee'. That is the way God puts it. And what is this but the emphasis of love? A lover is not content with sending one love-letter to his beloved, even if he can tell her everything that he can think of and that he feels. Before long he begins to have more things to say and he sends another such letter, and yet another. Love knows no scarcity of language. Out of the abundance of the heart the mouth is filled, and God, out of the abundance of His love, says, 'I will never, never, never leave you, and I will never, never forsake you'.

Put your own interpretation on this, and think of what all these 'nevers' might mean. They mean, for example, that He will never forsake you at any time. Perhaps last week you went to the bank and cashed a cheque and you got your money for it. Later the banker will send you the cheque that was duly cashed. Would you go to the bank with it again and ask the banker to give you cash a second time? Little good that would do you! Your cheque would not be cashed a second time; it was cashed once and for all. It is of no value for getting more money into your pocket. But that is not the way with the divine promise. A thousand different circumstances in the one day may cause you to come with this cheque, as it were, and God says all the time, 'I will never, never, never leave thee'. Oh, what a blessed God He is! How great is His love! You can come to Him as often as is necessary. You can come at any time. And you can come wherever you may be, and whether you are well or ill. Put more value on the presence of your God than on anything else.

I hope you do not live in fear of some calamity overtaking you, or of some disease attacking you. Learn so to live with God, relying on His promises, that these things will be secondary. A person may say, 'I am afraid I may get cancer'. Others may say, 'I am afraid I may have a heart attack and die'; or you may fear that certain troubles may come upon your family. Let these things be of minor importance. What does it matter when God says, 'I will never, never, never leave you'. Would you not rather be in the hospital dying of cancer, with this promise of God close to your heart, than be at home and well, desolate, hopeless and godless? Would you not rather be like Job, scraping himself because of his boils, yet with the promise of God and able to say, 'I know that my Redeemer liveth', than have all his possessions without his God? Ever remember and ever plead God's promise, 'I will never, never, never leave thee, and I will never, never forsake thee'.

I have said that God will never leave you on any occasion, but I wish to add a further word. You know that I give no encouragement to anybody to sin, and I am confident that what I am about to say will not be misinterpreted and misunderstood by a discerning Christian. My next word is this: even if you fall into sin, God will not forsake you. That is no encouragement to anyone to sin and it will not be taken as such by any real Christian. The divine promise is unconditional. He says, 'I will never, never, never leave thee, nor forsake thee'. Surely the promise will make you avoid sin. And yet we know that sin dogs our steps. If we are spared for another hour or minute, we know that we shall sin. We cannot avoid sinning. But then, God smiles upon His people in the end. Oh, He frowns, too, but His promises are true: 'I will never leave thee nor forsake thee'.

V THE PROOF OF THE PROMISE

How do we know that the promise is true? As I close I must speak a word on this matter. If you look into the history of the Church of

God, and can point out to me one believing soul – however obscure, however much of a backslider he became – if you can point out to me one Christian that God ever left or forsook, then everything that I have said goes for nothing. But you will never be able to point out one. Never! The whole history of the church is proof of His promise and of its fulfilment for you. The people of God have often been a stubborn people, a rebellious people, a sinful people; there have been sheep in the flock who went astray; there have been people who did evil. But the Lord never forsook one of them. And have not I therefore got the right to conclude and to say that He will never forsake me, if the mark of the blood of redemption is upon me? And then there is the matter of their acceptance with Christ Jesus: 'I will never leave thee'. Can God forsake Christ who is at His right hand? Can He shut Him out? Can He put Him out of heaven and exclude Him from the holy place? It is blasphemous to imagine it. It is an impossibility, and it is equally impossible that any true believer in Christ will be forsaken. If God will forsake you, then He will forsake Christ Jesus, for you are a member of His body, of His flesh and of His bones. You are part of Him. Christ owns you; you are not your own; you are written on His heart. If God forsakes *you*, then He will forsake Him. But He cannot forsake Him. Will not this truth stimulate your faith and silence your doubts and your fears? It is not blasphemy; I am trying to put the truth into strong language; God save me from blasphemy. But I say again, that the Father would just as soon exclude His own Son from His covenant blessings, as exclude you. You have a part in Christ. He is your Mediator and you have been accepted in Him.

And I must not fail to mention the all-prevailing intercession. What did Christ pray for? John 17 opens a door in heaven, as it were, and lets us know how Jesus intercedes for His own. In that chapter he gives us a specimen of what that intercession is: 'Father, I pray that thou wouldest keep those whom thou hast given me. I pray that they may be kept by thy name, by they truth. Father, I will that they whom thou hast given me be with me where I am, that they may see my glory'. This is the intercession of Christ, the all-prevailing intercession. Will God turn a deaf ear to the intercession of His son? Never, never! You could go on to multiply your 'nevers' till the end of time, and it will still be true, 'I will never leave thee nor forsake thee'. Ah, but you say, what I am afraid of is my death bed. What shall I be like when I come to die? I do not know what you will be like in that day. I do not know what your fears will be, any more than I know what mine will be, if we have time for reflection. Death may come suddenly. Or if we are lying prostrate on a bed of sickness for weeks and months on end and in pain I do not know what our feelings will be. But I know this, that if we are His He will never forsake us. And that suffices. Lay hold by faith of the wonderful promise that is our present theme; plead it in prayer; plead it as thanksgiving – 'I will never, never, never leave thee. I will never, never forsake thee' – and when you are received up into glory, prayer will be turned into praise. Amen and Amen.

∾ 13 ∾

The Marriage Supper of the Lamb

Let us be glad and rejoice, and give honour to him: for the marriage of the Lamb is come, and his wife hath made herself ready. And to her was granted that she should be arrayed in fine linen, clean and white: for the fine linen is the righteousness of saints. And he saith unto me, Write, Blessed are they which are called unto the marriage supper of the Lamb. And he saith unto me, These are the true sayings of God.

Revelation 19:7–9[1]

God has not only put faith in Himself and love to Him in the heart of all His people, but also the grace of hope in things that are to come. Some of these things are revealed to us in a measure in His Word, and on His Word our hopes are placed.

The hope of the Christian is not built on sentiment. When we talk about heaven, we should not talk about it in a sentimental way but as an eternal reality, for that is what it really is. Many people tend to think of heaven as a place where we shall meet our loved ones, where we shall have a reunion with those whom we loved by family ties, by natural relationship in this life. But in the next world there will be nothing like that. If we meet our wives and our husbands and our children and our parents we will not meet them as such, for in heaven they are like the angels of God who neither marry nor are given in marriage. We shall not lose our identity, but we shall certainly lose the kind of affection which binds us to people on this earth: that will be gone for ever. If you meet your child in glory, he or she will be to you like the child of anyone else, for the simple reason that natural relationships are no more. You will be in a new place, in a new world, where natural relationships are not. This should not sadden us. It may seem to you really hard

[1]April 5, 1975.

teaching, to be told that you will not see your loved ones. But I have not said that you will not see your loved ones. What I have said is that natural ties will be no more. Instead of being saddened as, humanly speaking, we are apt to be at this thought, it should be one of joy and gladness to us. Old things will be completely put away. As Jesus says, 'Behold, I make all things new' (*Rev. 21:5*).

I THE CONTENT OF THE SONG

The Word of God gives us insight into eternal realities. To those of us who love the Lord, who believe in Him and have hope in Him, a door into the future is opened. First of all, we learn that there will be a complete destruction of all evil. Whatever is meant by Babylon, the great whore, she is going to be destroyed for ever. I am not concerned about what is meant by Babylon. I do not intend to spend any time at all on that matter. I simply do not know. What matters to me is that I know from the Word of God that the day is coming when everything that represents evil, or whatever other name evil is called by in the Bible, is to be completely destroyed and cast into its own place. No place will be found for it in the presence of God, and I think that should be enough for us all. As we look upon the world today and as we think of the evil of it, in historical perspective, we wonder how it can be possible for there to be a world without sin, but God says it will be so, and what is more, we hope to be in it.

Now after the destruction of Babylon, that is, of all evil, honour and glory and power are ascribed unto God by the great multitude that will stand in His presence, for this is what we read: 'And I heard as it were the voice of a great multitude, and as the voice of many waters, and as the voice of mighty thunderings, saying, Alleluia: for the Lord God omnipotent reigneth' (*19:6*). When that time comes there will not be a discordant note; there will not be a division; there will not be different denominations as we see them today. We shall all be in the same place, and we shall not only be one with Christ Jesus, we shall be one *in* Christ Jesus, which is taking it a little further. We shall be one in Him as well as one with Him, and there will not be one discordant note in the whole heavenly choir. All will worship God and all will worship Him in the same way, and all the glory will be ascribed unto the Lord. He is the conductor (as it were) of the heavenly orchestra. In this Book of Revelation it is put in a wonderful way: 'And a voice came out of the throne, saying, Praise our God . . .' (*19:5*). What does this mean? We would not be surprised to read that voices were coming from around the throne, saying 'Praise our God'. But this voice came from the throne itself. And who is on the throne? The Lamb is on the throne. And out of the throne came a voice saying, 'Praise our God, all ye his servants, and ye that fear him, both small and great'. Here is that frequent identification of Christ with his people that we come across so often. He says, in the second chapter of Hebrews, verse 12, 'In the midst of the church will I sing praise unto thee'. And in this Christ is one with His people as He says in the verse which follows, 'Behold I and the children which God hath given me'.

Here, then, we read that a voice came out of the throne saying 'Praise our God'. It is the Mediator calling upon the host to praise, not your God, but 'our God.' And when we gather together in the heavenly mansions to ascribe praise and honour and glory to 'our God', the Leader, our Leader of praise, will be none other than our Lord and Saviour Jesus Christ, who is here referred to as the Lamb. He is God. He always was and never ceases to be God. But here He joins with His people and says, 'Praise our God'. Not because He is exhorted to do so! He bestows upon them (as it were) extra grace in order that they might sing louder to Him, 'Praise our God, all ye his servants, and ye that fear him, both small and great'. And the voice of the people praises Him with 'Amen' and 'Alleluia'. I doubt very much if the Amen was ever said in this world as it should have been said, except in the Garden of Gethsemane. We say it after every prayer. We ask petitions of God, in private and in public, and at the end of these petitions we say 'Amen', which means 'So be it' or 'Let thy will be done'. But do we really mean it? Do we really say 'Amen' to all our petitions put before God?

John Newton wrote a hymn in which he asks God to sanctify him, to make him holier and more like Himself, and he proceeds to tell how God touched him and put a crown of thorns on him. That was how God answered his prayer. And when we say 'Sanctify me, make me holier, make me like Christ', and God proceeds to do it by the tearing off of a limb, or the plucking out of an eye, is our 'Amen' one hundred per cent genuine? Speaking for myself, I am afraid mine is not; far more, I know that it is not. But when we remember Gethsemane, we see there the God-man Christ in terrible agony and conflict, crying, 'Father, if it be possible, let this cup pass from me,' and then saying 'Not as I will, but as thou wilt'. And in heaven everyone will be in full agreement with the will and the wisdom and the holiness of God. The word 'Alleluia' is only found in this book in the Bible, but it is the same as 'Praise the Lord', words which occur so often in the Old Testament. So in heaven there is holy and complete acquiescence mixed with holy and consistent praise.

This kind of praise is something that is not heard in this world. We do not find it in the church militant, for unmixed and complete agreement and acquiescence in the will of God without the slightest reservation is an utterly impossible thing for anyone who has the least vestige of sin in his heart. But in the church triumphant sin will be altogether taken away, and there all believers will be for ever in full agreement with the will of God. When they say, 'Alleluia, Praise the Lord', it is the response of all holy hearts to all that God is. It is the response in fulness of what we feel and know only in part in this world. I am not referring merely to our feelings. On the other hand, I am not saying that the people of God in this world have not feelings. They certainly have feelings, and sometimes in the public means of grace and in the private means of grace, sitting at the Lord's Table or listening to the gospel, we feel a response in our hearts, a response of adoration and affection towards God that cannot be accounted for in any other way but by the fact that the Holy Spirit has put it into us. I am as sure of that as that I am standing in your presence. We get evidences within ourselves, invisibly and secretly, by our private and inward and secret response that we are His. 'The Spirit beareth witness with our spirit that we are the children of God' (*Rom. 8:16*).

II THE OCCASION OF THE SONG

Thus far we have looked at the content of the song but I want to turn your attention also to the occasion of the song. Here is the announcement of a royal marriage. 'Let us be glad and rejoice, and give honour to him: for the marriage of the Lamb is come, and his wife hath made herself ready'. The analogy, like every other analogy, is imperfect, but it is illustrative, though not in every sense. The marriage of the Lamb came long before this: it happens in the world, not in heaven. The marriage of the Lamb to His bride, or to His wife, happens only in this world. I know you all agree with me, but there are many who think they have what they call a second chance, but there will be no 'second chance', and the righteous and necessary relationship between Christ and those who will be with Him in glory must be formed here, not there. We must by faith embrace Him. He receives us unto Himself and by faith we embrace Him as our Saviour. We must embrace Him by faith as our Husband in this world. A vital union is made between us, in the faith in which we are born again, that will never be dissolved. 'Neither death, nor life, nor angels, nor principalities, nor powers, nor things present, nor things to come, shall be able to separate us from the love of God, which is in Christ Jesus our Lord' (*Rom. 8:38–39*).

I spoke to you of the changelessness of His love recently – 'I have loved thee with an everlasting love; therefore with lovingkindness have I drawn thee', and I need not now enlarge upon it. The closest union in this world can be broken, as many of you know by bitter experience. Death has no mercy, the grave knows no pity. But there is one thing over which death has no power, and that is the union that exists between Christ and the regenerate soul. And that union begins in this world. The marriage is made here and not there, so in that sense the marriage of the Lamb has already come. Remember this also that insofar as relationship is concerned, you will not be any nearer related to Christ in heaven than you are at this very moment if you are a Christian. You cannot be nearer related to Christ than you are now. It cannot be nearer or closer than it is at this very moment. He will be nearer to you by way of location, but not by way of contract. The marriage contract has already been entered into and it cannot be closer. I agree that we shall be closer by way of condition; that is, our own condition will be changed; we shall have spiritual bodies, sinless bodies and sinless souls. In the resurrection glory the body of our humiliation will be made like unto His glorious body, but in contract and relationship we are here and now in eternal union with our Lord.

'The marriage of the Lamb is come and his wife hath made herself ready'. One of the sweetest names by which the church of Christ is known in the New Testament is that of the bride and one of the sweetest names by which He is known is that of the Bridegroom. You know what the word 'bride' means in our language. We see the bride coming down the aisle and the bridegroom is waiting for her. They are about to be married, but she is not yet his wife; she is the bride, who is about to become his wife. So, as I say, the analogy is not complete: the bride of the Lamb is the wife of the Lamb. But for a moment let us think of it in our own usual way. As we go through this life as a Christian church our Bridegroom is absent. He married us to Himself and then He went away. He went away to the palace, to the mansion of His Father and He left us in this world to fight the conflicts of life, the good fight of faith, to wage the warfare of the Christian. He left us to tread in His footsteps, but we do not see Him, we have never seen Him. The vale of time is between us. We see Him by faith, but we have never seen Him with our natural eyes. But there, we shall see Him face to face, and His name shall be in our foreheads. And there we shall see Him as the Lamb of God, and that is full of significance. This name was given to Him from all eternity, a name that was given to Him in token of sacrifice, a name that was given to Him by John the Baptist, greatest of the prophets, and a name that has followed Him even to the right hand of the Father in glory. And so shall we follow Him as the bride of the Lamb. But in the meantime, as I say, we go through this life. As it were, the bride is waiting for the marriage day. Or, if I may put it perhaps in a better way, we have already been married to Him but the reception has not come. The day of the reception is awaiting us; it is certain to come. And this is a wonderful thing, I think, whichever way we look at it; it is marvellous to the extreme. There we shall see Him, face to face.

Rabbi Duncan once said, 'Next to the sight of the Lamb, I would like to see His bride'. For there is nothing in heaven more precious than the bride (or the wife of the Lamb) except the Lamb Himself. She is more precious than the angels, and if I may say so, she is more loved than the angels, for she is the Lamb's wife. She is more honoured than the angels. I remember in my student days, there was a girl in Glasgow, whom I knew among other Christians: God took her away to glory when she was but young and near to God in her walk and conversation. I remember her telling on one occasion how somebody said in her hearing, 'Well, if I get to heaven, I would like to be a servant to the angels', and she answered, 'My dear girl, if you ever get to heaven, the angels will be servants to you'. She knew her Bible; she was quite right. We shall not, friends, be servants to the angels, but as they are our ministering spirits here, they shall be our ministering spirits there. So next to the Lamb there is the wife of the Lamb.

'The marriage of the Lamb is come' – the reception, the marriage feast – 'and his wife hath made herself ready'. There is one thing which I must say concerning it. Not one will be absent of those that are described as His wife, not one. As a believer you may have been a fretting, captious, rebellious one, and although I say it with shame, you may have been an unfaithful wife to Him. Still, you will be there, all will be forgiven and you will be there. Nothing will keep you back. I was at a marriage, not long ago in Inverness: it was the marriage of a person from the West Coast and there were lots of telegrams read at the reception, many of them read like this, 'Regret we cannot be with you: Stormbound'. There were terrific gales in the islands on the west coast and the ferries were not running. How different from the situation here! We have our storms; you know what they are; you know what the afflictions of life are like; you know the agony of heart and the sorrow and the tears, when others are asleep; you know the conflict with sin. But think of these storms not as keeping you from the port, not as hindering you from getting to the reception, but instead as being used to waft you on, to drive you towards where the Bridegroom is awaiting you. Paul says, 'All things work together for good to them that love God' (*Rom. 8:28*) – storms and all, they work together for our good, and they draw us nearer to the reception. We are nearer to it today than we were yesterday! There are things in time, sent by the wisdom of God to help us on, to make us walk forward, to loosen our affection from the world.

Blessed be God for afflictions! God knows that we have hearts that are bound to this earth and God loosens them from it. He comes and He hurts our fingers, He hurts our affections. He hurts us in many ways in order to loosen us from the grasp of this wicked world, to conform us to Himself. 'The marriage of the Lamb is come and his wife hath made herself ready'. That does not mean that she has any hand in her justification or in her sanctification. Both belong to Him and are His work. But I think it means an entire willingness on her part, this is what I meant by the 'Amen' to which I referred earlier. I think it means credit for the endeavours that she has made in the world to be like Him. In the Bible God has made it known that our works are not meritorious in the least; nothing of ours has any merit. But, if you look at your Bibles carefully you will notice that God, as it were, deals with us as if these things meant much, and every endeavour you make after holiness is recorded in the annals of heaven. 'His wife hath made herself ready'. That is the readiness for which we are waiting: that is the readiness for which we are working: that is the readiness for which we are praying.

III THE MARRIAGE FEAST

Next, what will the feast be like? It will be public and it will be glorious. I have spoken about conflicts, but the conflicts and the famines will make the feast more glorious. An abundance of food is of no use to a full soul, but it is God's will to lead His wife through the wilderness where she often experiences the pangs of hunger. One saint of God said, 'Oh that I knew where I might find Him; that I might come even to his seat'. Another said, 'They have taken away my Lord and I know not where they have laid Him'. She had lost Him and she did not know where to find Him. That is what the wife says in the Song of Solomon, 'I sought him but I could not find him; I called him but he gave me no answer'. What did she seek after? She would be fed on love, fed on His love to her and we may even say fed on her love to Him. What a feast it will be!

I do not know what your present feelings may be, but I would not be at all surprised if some of you are afraid that you will never reach glory. You are afraid that the ring you wear is not His gift; you are afraid that the dress you have on is not His righteousness: you are afraid that the marriage certificate has not been signed by Him, and therefore is not valid. But banish your fears, banish them all. The ring you have *is* His, He gave it to you. He put it on your finger. Who else could put it on? And the dress you wear is His righteousness, clean and white. Who else had it to give you? This is the marriage dress woven by Him with hands imbrued with blood, His pierced hands. Oh what a precious garment it is! Who else could give you a garment like it? Who else could give you a garment, won and paid for by substitution, by being forsaken of the Father on the cross? Do not be afraid; trust fully in your Lord. His name is on your certificate also, as well as your own. His name is on it as sure and surer even than yours and if your name is on it, it is because His name was on it first. And at the feast we shall see Him.

There is something wonderful here and I must explain it to you. The more fellowship we get with Christ in the world, the more ashamed we feel in His presence. There is no one more ashamed of himself in the presence of the Lord than the person who is nearest to Him. How we can look upon Him, how we can see Him face to face, as we see one another just now, without being ashamed, I cannot tell, for it is an experience we have never had in this world. But that is how it is going to be. We shall see Him. We shall have humility without shame in His presence. We shall look upon Him and we shall not be ashamed nor will there be misunderstanding or disagreement. There will be no parting. There will be no divisions. There will be no devil. Oh, what havoc he has caused in the church! How he has set brethren one against the other, denomination against denomination! But they shall come from the north and from the south, from the east and from the west, and they shall sit together as one in the Kingdom of God.

I would plead with you in His name. Try to be as like His wife as you possibly can be. Try to get her disposition as much as you possibly can, even while you are here on earth. Seek to have His disposition here in part, which you will have in full there. Blessed are they who are invited to the marriage supper of the Lamb. Blessed indeed are they!

There are two things remaining. First of all, I would speak a word to unbelievers. How can you possibly contain your grief at not being one of the Lord's people, at not being the wife of the Lamb? How can you possibly live without being the wife of Christ? How is it that grief does not break your heart that you are not the wife of Christ?

To the believer I would say, How can you contain your joy, your joy of anticipation as well as your joy of fellowship at being His wife? 'I reckon', said Paul, 'that the sufferings of this present time are not worthy to be compared with the glory which shall be revealed in us' (*Rom. 8:18*). As I was thinking upon these things, I decided to close my address with words written by a German hymn-writer named Tersteegen and translated into English by Frances Bevan. It seems to me to be one of the most beautiful hymns ever written. It speaks of the subject of my address, and the

verses I will quote will close the service far better than any words of
mine. It speaks of the bride reaching the realm of glory:

> *Midst the darkness, storm and sorrow*
> *One bright gleam I see;*
> *Well I know the blessed morrow –*
> *Christ will come for me.*
>
> *Midst the light and peace and glory*
> *Of the Father's home,*
> *Christ for me is watching, waiting,*
> *Waiting till I come.*
>
> *Oh, the blessed joy of meeting –*
> *All the desert past:*
> *Oh, the wondrous words of greeting*
> *He shall speak at last!*
>
> *He and I in that bright glory*
> *One deep joy shall share:*
> *Mine, to be for ever with Him,*
> *His, that I am there!*

๑๑ 14 ๑๑

Heaven: the Lamb Adored

And I beheld, and, lo, in the midst of the throne and of the four beasts and in the midst of the elders, stood a Lamb as it had been slain, having seven horns and seven eyes, which are the seven Spirits of God sent forth into all the earth.

Revelation 5:6[1]

It might be profitable to refer back to the preceding chapter in order to get a clearer view of the context of our text. In the revelations made to him, John saw a throne and Him who sat upon it 'was to look upon like a jasper and a sardine stone'. Round about the throne were four and twenty seats, and upon the seats four and twenty elders sitting. Next John saw four living beasts full of eyes before and behind. One was like a lion, another like a calf, the third like a man, and the fourth like a flying eagle. Now all this is figurative, of course. It points to the united church of Christ. Now it goes without saying that the church of Christ is without seam. God never rent the church; we have done that. He did not mean us to do it, nor did He want us to do it, but we did it in various ways including dissensions and controversies. But in the sight of God there is only one church, and it little matters what denomination a person belongs to if he is united by faith to Jesus Christ and is thereby a Christian. He is a member of the church of God. Now that goes without saying.

The four and twenty elders are representatives of Christ's united church. We may ask, 'Why twenty-four? Why not twenty?' Twenty-four is twice twelve; there were twelve tribes in Israel and there were twelve Apostles. The figure may therefore signify the

[1]March 6, 1977. This was Mr. MacDonald's last evening service at Greyfriars before his death on April 15.

[134]

union of the Testaments or better still, the union of the redeemed, both Jews and Gentiles. The Old Testament dispensation was confined exclusively to the Jews. Not so the New
Testament. In the New Testament we read how the Gentiles also
received the Word of God. Other interpretations are sometimes
given but I state the best I know.

Then too, there were four living creatures, the word being
unfortunately translated in our version as 'beasts'. But they were
four living 'beings'. They represent the union of the creation of
God, in worship; they all fall down and worship Him who sits
upon the throne. Notice their characteristics. One was like a lion
– an animal characterized by bravery. Another was like an ox –
signifying the characteristic of patience. Another was like an
eagle and its characteristic is aspiration, it seems. The fourth had
a face like a man, and what distinguishes a man from the other
living creatures that are upon the earth is his intelligence. So you
have these four things blended together in the worship of God –
holy boldness, courage, in the service of God; patience to endure
trials and to wait for the Lord's coming; aspiration in the pursuit
of holiness; and finally intelligence enlightened by the Holy
Spirit. And the four are united in falling down before the throne,
and before the Lamb in worship. That is the background of the
text.

Now the text itself is one of the most beautiful in the Bible. 'I
beheld, and, lo, a Lamb as it had been slain. . . .' In the context
we have a passage brimful of theology and doctrine. In fact, the
beauty of the passage, and of the English, and of the figures used,
might even tend to blind us to the doctrines which are contained
in it. There are two doctrines in particular to which I wish to
draw your attention, and to refer particularly to the finer points
of theology that I find in them.

First of all we see here the doctrine of the Trinity – three
persons, but one God. One person was sitting on the throne, One
person was not sitting on the throne but standing in the midst,
and there was One who had seven eyes which are the seven
Spirits of God. Here we see plainly the doctrine of the Triune
God – the Trinity. The One sitting on the throne is God the
Father; the one standing in the midst is God the Son, the Lamb;
and the seven Spirits (and the figure seven indicates perfection)
means the Holy Ghost.

Secondly, we have the three offices of Christ. As we read about Christ in the Scriptures we find much mention of His three offices. He is Prophet, Priest and King. All that Christ has done or is doing for His church is contained within these three offices. Theologians systematize things for us in this way, and it is perfectly right and exceedingly good and useful. Christ is a King because He is in the midst of the throne; He is the centre of rule and authority in the place of glory. He is a Priest; this is indicated in the name Lamb which is given to Him. A lamb was commonly used in the sacrificial offering. He is a Prophet because He came and took the book out of the hand of Him who sat on the throne; and the office of the prophet was to read the law of God to the people, and interpret and proclaim it to them. So we have the three offices of Christ in this passage. Notice them particularly.

I WHY JOHN WEPT

We come now to the words of chapter 5. John saw in the hand of Him who sat on the throne a book sealed, or rather a scroll, for there were no books, as we know them, in those days. Writings were on scrolls and they were rolled up and sealed. This scroll was sealed with seven seals, again the number for perfection, and then it was said that no one was worthy to open the book or to loose the seals of it. What book was it? The book was in the hand of God the Father, who sat on the throne. What does that indicate? According to those who tell us the meaning of these things (and I think we ourselves could quite easily get the same meaning out of it), it is the book of the secret counsels of God both in grace and in providence. For the sake of convenience we usually distinguish between the realm of grace and the realm of providence, but they are actually the same. They are not two distinct realms, for there is no dividing line between the grace of God and the providence of God. He works in them equally and is the sole worker in them. So it is merely for the sake of convenience that I speak both of grace and providence.

Here then is a book which symbolizes the secret counsels of God in grace and providence. You know how secret is providence. We do not know what will happen on the morrow. But God knows. The prophets of old did not know when Christ was coming. They knew that He *was* coming, but none of them knew the time of His coming. That was in the secret counsels of God, and when they prophesied, Peter himself tells us that they themselves searched into their prophecies, into their own inspired sayings, to find out the meaning of the words they themselves had uttered by the Holy Spirit. But here in chapter 5 of the Book of Revelation is a book which cannot be opened or searched by any man.

John next tells us that he beheld a strong angel who cried saying, 'Who is worthy to open the book?' I do not know what is the special force of the adjective 'strong' in this verse. 'A strong angel'. Every angel is strong. Probably John means an angel stronger than other angels because there is an hierarchy of angels. There are some nearer the throne than others. It seems to me that it is one of the chiefest of angels who asked the question, 'Who is worthy to open the book and to loose the seven seals thereof?' Sometimes people quote the verse wrongly, saying, 'Who is *able* to open the book', but that is not what the angel said. His words ran, 'Who is *worthy* to open the book?' It was not a question of power or strength, as much as a question of moral stature. A person may be able, by reason of strength to do something and be quite unworthy morally to do it. This, then, is the point that is brought out: Who is *worthy* to open the book? And there was no-one, John tells us, among either angels or men, in heaven or in earth, who was able (in the moral sense) to open the book or loose the seals thereof. It is clear that no creature was morally worthy to approach the throne and Him who sat on it. We know that the angels are perfectly holy and that the saints who were in glory when John had the vision, were perfectly holy, but they were not worthy to open the book, either singly or collectively. No one was worthy to open the book. In other words, in a comparative sense, no one is worthy to approach the throne of God. It is far above even the highest of angels. Not even the strong angel who asked the question could do it. 'Who is worthy?' he said. That is, the angel himself did not know and could not find an answer to the problem.

John 'wept much', not out of curiosity, but because there was no one able to open the book or loose the seals thereof. Curiosity is a weakness of ours; we would fain find out things God did not mean to tell us. 'Are there few that be saved?' said a man to Christ when He was on the earth. And Christ replied, 'Strive to enter in at the strait gate', implying that the inquiry was quite out of place

(*Luke 13:24*). The question is not relevant, it is not necessary to answer it. Christ never left a question unanswered that was relevant, He always gave a straight answer. He did so to the man who asked Him, 'Which is the greatest of the commandments?' Jesus replied, 'Thou shalt love the Lord thy God with all thy heart, and with all thy soul, and with all thy mind' (*Matt. 22:37*). He went further and told the man that there was a second commandment like unto it: 'Thou shalt love thy neighbour as thyself'. That was the Lord's manner, but with questions arising from curiosity He would have nothing to do. Herod was desirous of a long time to see Jesus and when they met he asked Him many questions but He answered him nothing. He would not satisfy Herod's curiosity. Curiosity is a human weakness; we want to pry into the affairs of one another and there are some people who make a great nuisance of themselves in that respect. They would even pry into the secrets of the Godhead, the secret counsels of God. People ask the most silly questions regarding heaven and hell. Even if they had the right answer it would not help them or sanctify them.

John 'wept much', says the Scripture (*Rev. 5:4*). Why did he weep? He wept out of concern for what was to happen to the world if the book was not opened. He understood that the destiny of the world depended on the book being opened and the seals being loosed. And there was no one worthy to do it. John saw, as it were, the world completely lost and undone, in complete ruin, because no-one was able to open the book. He understood that in that scroll there was the answer to the world's problems of sin, the answer to the question, 'How can a man be just with God?' but the book was sealed and John wept out of concern for the destiny of his fellow-men. If the book remained sealed the world would be lost. And the weeping was not something that was confined to John. Men and women whom God has greatly used in the world have wept out of real concern for their fellow-men. John Knox, John Welsh, Charles Haddon Spurgeon, and, to go back to a greater than any of them, Paul, all wept tears of real concern. And my brothers and sisters, Christian believers, I wonder if you ever wept over the souls of other people. If you turn to *The Confessions of Augustine*, you will read of the tears of his mother Monica at the thought of her son, living in sin and perishing. In his book Augustine tells us that his mother wept over him, over the state of his soul, more than any mother could weep over the death of her child.

[138]

John 'wept much'. And then one of the elders said to him, 'Weep not; behold, the Lion of the tribe of Juda, the Root of David, hath prevailed to open the book and to loose the seven seals thereof'. How did He prevail to open the book? How does a lion prevail in the hunt? By strength and courage, for he is the king of beasts. But how did 'the Lion of the tribe of Juda' prevail? Think of Christ in Gethsemane; remember how He sweated blood out of weakness and mental anguish, how He gave Himself over to be apprehended and bound, how He was taken to the High Priest and to the Governor, how He was crucified. He was brought as a Lamb to the slaughter yet He opened not His mouth. When He was reviled, He reviled not again. The Lion of the tribe of Judah prevailed to open the book by weakness, by humiliation, by gentleness, by patience, by pain, by shame, and by death itself. There was omnipotence behind it, we know, else He could never have accomplished the work that the Father gave Him to do. But what was being manifested to the eyes of men was not omnipotency but the gentleness of the Lamb, 'a Lamb as it had been slain' (*v. 6*).

One of the elders said to John, 'Weep not!'. How applicable this is to ourselves on many occasions. I know that some of you from time to time wet your pillow with your tears. It is a strange thing if we can go through life without getting something to weep about. Sooner or later troubles and trials come to us all. But here the elder said to John: 'Your tears are unnecessary. The Lion of the tribe of Judah wept, and because He wept you do not need to weep. He wept and by so doing He prevailed to open the book.' Mary and Martha wept when Jesus came to the tomb of Lazarus. That was perfectly natural. It is often the case that when a friend visits people who have had a bereavement, it causes them to shed a flood of tears. That is what happened at Bethany. Their dear friend who had been absent and was sent for came at last and they wept. But their tears, although they were absolutely natural, were also absolutely unnecessary. The Lord Himself would weep at the grave of Lazarus, and because of His tears the two sisters did not need to weep at all. But they were ignorant of this. If they had known they would not have wept.

But let me apply this to ourselves. It is perfectly natural to weep out of heartfelt sorrow, and it is not a sin to do so, but if only we knew the end of the Lord, we should also know that many of our tears are unnecessary. Job wept, for he did not know the end, the design of the Lord. All things work together for good to those who love Him. And if you knew the desire, the plan of God for you, you would rejoice rather than be sad. 'Weep not'! What words these are to the believer! Responding to the elder's words, John looked and he saw in the midst of the throne 'a Lamb as it had been slain'. Here Christ is in the place of eminence and of authority but He is not sitting on the throne. He is acting as Mediator. Christ is said, now, not to be on the throne. The Bible does not say anywhere that He is on the throne as God. He is at the right hand of God but that is said of Him as Mediator, not as God. It is said of Him as God and man. But there is a time coming when Christ will cease to act as Mediator and he will hand the kingdom over to His Father, that God may be all in all. The Mediatorial kingdom of Christ will have an end. Christ will cease to intercede and then He will not be at the right hand of God, but He will hand over the kingdom to that God, the three persons, not God the Father alone.

II THE LAMB SLAIN

John tells us that he saw 'a Lamb as it had been slain'. The Greek word John uses here for 'a Lamb' is not used in Scripture outside the Book of Revelation. For example, when John the Baptist said, 'Behold the Lamb of God', another word is used. What John the Baptist used was the usual word for a lamb, but the word used by the Apostle John in Revelation means 'little lamb'. It is a diminutive. 'I beheld, and lo . . . stood a little Lamb'. All this is full of significance for us, for it shows us the glory of what is going to follow. The term 'little lamb' is used for our encouragement, and to spur us on in our adoration of the One who is both able and worthy to take the book out of the hand of Him who sits on the throne.

John saw 'a lamb as it had been slain', the marks of wounds were upon the Lamb. If we ask whether Christ bears the scar of the nails, the print of the nails, in His hands and in His feet, in heaven, we are in the realm of curiosity and speculation. It is a question that we should never ask. John had earlier seen the print of the nails; certainly they were in His resurrection body. He had said to Thomas, 'Reach hither thy finger and behold my hands' (*John*

20:27). The wounds were in His resurrection body after He rose from the dead. But to say that these wounds are in His glorified body in heaven is another matter entirely. I would not say that for all the world. If we think of Christ in a fleshly way, that is not the exercise of faith at all. The believer should not be concerned to know whether or not the wounds are on His body in heaven. The faith of the believer is based on Christ's work in history. 'He was wounded for our transgressions' and that is enough for faith. 'He was bruised for our iniquities: the chastisement of our peace was upon him; and with his stripes we are healed' (*Isa. 53:5*). That is where faith exercises itself, that is where it rests. Do not ask whether there are, or are not, marks upon His glorified body; if the thought comes into your mind, dismiss it for it is altogether improper. But it is Christ who died; John saw the 'Lamb as it had been slain'.

A Lamb who had not been slain would not have been worthy to approach the throne of God, and to take the book and open it. John saw a 'Lamb as it *had been slain*' – it is by virtue of His death, by virtue of His victory, that He is worthy to take the book and open it. Sometimes you hear it said that Christ is the power of God, and a passage in Corinthians is quoted – 'Christ the power of God and the wisdom of God'. But you must look at the words in the context in which they were written (*1 Cor. 1:24*). The Christ that Paul is there speaking about is Christ Jesus and Him crucified. That is the Christ he is talking about. Christ, in Himself, is not the power of God to the elect, for their salvation. It is Christ crucified who is the power of God unto the elect, for salvation. Christ crucified is the power of God and that is the kernel of the gospel. It is the Lamb, by virtue of having been slain, who is worthy to open the book and loose the seals thereof. This truth implies everything that is connected with the atonement; it implies the love of God, the wisdom of God, the power of God, the justice of God, the mercy of God. Furthermore, Christ is set before us as the object of our faith and admiration and love. Who is the object of your faith? Why do you believe your soul is saved and that you will never be lost? My plain, simple answer is this, 'It is Christ that died'. He died for me. My soul is saved, not because there is a second person in the Godhead, but because He died for me. A 'Lamb as it had been slain' is the object of my faith. You ask also, 'Why do you love Him?' I answer: 'I love Him because He was slain for me. I love

Him because He first loved me. Because He loved me, He died for me. Also, He is the object of my hope. The "Lamb as it had been slain" is coming back again.'

We speak truth: Christ is coming back again. To men and women who are not believers, His second coming will be far more terrible than earthquakes and other such disasters. The sun shall be turned into blood, the seas will be dried up, the dead shall be raised, the elements shall melt with fervent heat. The truth that Christ is coming again is enough to strike terror into the hearts of all; yes and to devils also, who tremble at the thought of the consummation when Jesus will come again to wind up all things. But if you are a Christian, you do not need to be terrified. It is the 'Lamb as it had been slain' who is coming, and He is your hope and the object of your hope. It is for you that He was slain. He is coming as your Friend. He is coming as your Saviour to take you to Himself.

III THE LAMB ADORED

The Book of Revelation also tells us that the Lamb came and took the book out of the hand of Him who sat on the throne. He looked on the book. Nobody else was worthy to look on it. He must have looked on it before He took it. Then He opened the book to make known unto us what it contained. It contained the purposes of God concerning His people, that they would be saved and they would never perish and no man would pluck them out of His hand. He was a party to all that was written in the book and He knew it. As our Mediator He possesses delegated knowledge and power. He Himself said, 'All power is given unto me in heaven and in earth' (*Matt. 28:18*). And what is the result? The adoration of the Lamb! And this I would say, that all that I have been saying is of no use whatsoever unless you go out of this house tonight, falling down, as it were, prostrating yourself before the Lord and praising Him as did those who said, 'Blessing and honour and glory and power be unto Him who sitteth upon the throne, and unto the Lamb for ever and ever'.

Sometimes Jehovah's Witnesses arrive at your door and they come to degrade Christ. They tell you that He is God's Son, that He is God's first-begotten, that He was first of all. But they also say that He had a beginning and that He is not God. The next time they come to your door and deny the deity of the Lord Jesus tell them that in this Book of Revelation the same adoration is ascribed to the 'Lamb as it had been slain' as is ascribed to Him who sat on the throne. Direct them to verse 13 of chapter 5: 'And every creature which is in heaven, and on the earth, and under the earth, and such as are in the sea, and all that are in them, heard I saying, Blessing, and honour, and glory, and power, be unto him that sitteth upon the throne, and unto the Lamb for ever and ever.' There is not a thing that is ascribed to God who sits on the throne, that is not ascribed to the 'Lamb as it had been slain'. Not one thing! They have the same honour and glory and blessing and power ascribed to them. Why? Because the Lamb as it had been slain, is God equally with the Father and the Holy Spirit. The adoration we give to the Lamb is of the same nature as the adoration we give to God the Father, but it is not for the same reason. Notice the words: 'And they sang a new song saying, Thou art worthy to take the book and to open the seals thereof; for thou wast slain, and hast redeemed us to God by thy blood, out of every kindred, and tongue, and people and nation'. The 'Lamb as it had been slain' is adored because He redeemed us by His own blood; that is the cause for adoration. But the nature of the adoration is just the same.

In drawing to a close, I call attention to this: that to fall before the throne, to show humility, reverence for the Lamb, and also to adore Him – these things are an infallible mark and evidence of having an interest in Christ. I do not know what you think of yourselves. I suppose that if you are right with God, you think of yourselves as poor sinners. But let me tell you this: that if tonight you are happy before God, and you *adore* Jesus Christ because you believe He redeemed you, you have an infallible evidence of grace. This adoration of Christ and of God is the first evidence of faith. It is the first evidence of grace in your soul. It is the first exercise of divine light in your soul. How do you act when you look at Jesus and when you see Him as the 'Lamb as it had been slain'? You adore Him as your God, you worship Him as your God. When, even for the first time, you look to Christ by faith, however weak your faith may be, you fall down and worship Him. You worship Him because He is your God. You worship God the Father through Him, but you worship Him equally with the Father. His work on our behalf makes our love flow out to Him. He becomes the supreme object of our love. He has won our wills to Himself. He has captivated, in a holy way, our hearts; He has taken our hearts to be His own. He has captivated our affections and made them His; no wonder, then, that we fall down and adore Him who stands in the midst of the throne of God.

One final word in parting. As a church, you know where we go wrong – it does not matter what church we belong to, this is true of us all – we go wrong when we put the Lamb out of His proper place, out of the midst. That is where His heart is; that is where He wishes to be and where He promised to be. To put Him out of His proper place is what the Corinthians did in the days of Paul. Some of them said, 'I am of Christ'; some said, 'I am of Paul'; others of Apollos, others of Cephas (Peter), and Paul says to them in searching words, as if they were words of fire, 'Was Paul crucified for you?' (*1 Cor. 1:13*). They were putting Jesus out of their midst. I want to say to you, do not put Jesus out of the midst of your heart tonight. Let Him be the centre to which everything in your life will gravitate. Otherwise, I would question very much whether you are a Christian at all. Christ must be, and continue to be, the centre of all things in your life. There are other things claiming to get into the midst of your heart – greed (Oh, the greed of the present age in which we live!), worldliness, love of the world, love of its ease, love of its luxuries, love of its plenty, love of its money, love of every kind other than love of Christ. This I say, that nothing is worthy of supreme love but Christ. There are people who are worthy of being loved much, but nothing and nobody is worthy of your *supreme* love but Christ alone. Do not let anyone have it but Christ alone. And, if you have a saving interest in Him, no one else will have your heart. Your faith will go out in adoration of Him as the 'Lamb as it had been slain', and your faith will exercise itself upon Him, manifesting itself in glorious adoration as long as you live. It will merge into an everlasting homage, after you leave this world and go into the next.

Let us pray:

'*O Lord, we pray that the Lamb crucified may be all in all unto us. There are some here, tonight, among us and Christ is to them as a root out of a dry ground. To them He means nothing, He is despised and utterly rejected of them. And there are some among us who, we believe, will go outside these doors rejecting Christ, the Lamb who was slain from the foundation of the world. But we thank thee that there are many among us who have been enabled by Thy grace to receive Him, to believe in Him, to love Him and adore Him. And now, Lord, we pray that a great change may come upon us all. Those who have never adored Him before, may then begin adoring Him now, and those of us who hope that we have been adoring Him, may we do so more and more, for His name's sake.* AMEN.

APPENDIX

Raigmore Hospital.

6th January, 1973

My beloved Congregation,

As you already know it has been God's will in the meantime to take me away from serving you in the active ministry. How long or short this will be He alone knows. During my 14 years as your minister this is the first time I was really ill, and we have reason to thank God for this.

During these years God has blessed us abundantly. Many souls we believe were brought to Jesus and His sheep and lambs have often sat at His feet listening to His Word. These were years of peace, unity and love between minister and people both in church and in your homes. No relation between a minister and people could be more amiable and confidential than ours has been.

God's saving power in the preaching of the Word does in no way depend on the preacher. It is therefore my daily prayer that many of you who listened to me with pleasure but who were not saved under my ministry, will receive a saving blessing from those who preach in my absence. If this is so, I will rejoice as much as them and you.

I am sure you will be as loyal and faithful in my absence as you were in my presence. In this way you will encourage the Elders who have such a responsibility at present upon them.

Finally, I am glad to tell you that my medical reports so far have been very favourable, and I am assured that after a safe period of rest I can lead a normal life of active ministry among you again.

May I have a place in your prayers as you have in mine.

Your affectionate Minister,

Donald MacDonald.